Hebrews

INTERPRETATION
A Bible Commentary for Teaching and Preaching

INTERPRETATION

A BIBLE COMMENTARY FOR TEACHING AND PREACHING

James Luther Mays, *Editor*
Patrick D. Miller Jr., *Old Testament Editor*
Paul J. Achtemeier, *New Testament Editor*

Old Testament: *Genesis* by Walter Brueggemann
Exodus by Terence E. Fretheim
Leviticus by Samuel E. Balentine
Numbers by Dennis T. Olson
Deuteronomy by Patrick D. Miller
Joshua by Jerome F. D. Creach
Judges by J. Clinton McCann
Ruth by Katharine Doob Sakenfeld
First and Second Samuel by Walter Brueggemann
First and Second Kings by Richard D. Nelson
First and Second Chronicles by Steven S. Tuell
Ezra–Nehemiah by Mark A. Throntveit
Esther by Carol M. Bechtel
Job by J. Gerald Janzen
Psalms by James L. Mays
Proverbs by Leo G. Perdue
Ecclesiastes by William P. Brown
Song of Songs by Robert W. Jenson
Isaiah 1–39 by Christopher R. Seitz
Isaiah 40–66 by Paul D. Hanson
Jeremiah by R. E. Clements
Lamentations by F. W. Dobbs-Allsopp
Ezekiel by Joseph Blenkinsopp
Daniel by W. Sibley Towner
Hosea–Micah by James Limburg
Nahum–Malachi by Elizabeth Achtemeier

New Testament: *Matthew* by Douglas R. A. Hare
Mark by Lamar Williamson Jr.
Luke by Fred B. Craddock
John by Gerard S. Sloyan
Acts by William H. Willimon
Romans by Paul J. Achtemeier
First Corinthians by Richard B. Hays
Second Corinthians by Ernest Best
Galations by Charles Cousar
Ephesians, Colossians, and Philemon by Ralph. P. Martin
Philippians by Fred B. Craddock
First and Second Thessalonians by Beverly Roberts Gaventa
First and Second Timothy and Titus by Thomas C. Oden
Hebrews by Thomas G. Long
First and Second Peter, James, and Jude by Pheme Perkins
First, Second, and Third John by D. Moody Smith
Revelation by M. Eugene Boring

THOMAS G. LONG

Hebrews

INTERPRETATION

A Bible Commentary
for Teaching and Preaching

WESTMINSTER
JOHN KNOX PRESS
LOUISVILLE • KENTUCKY

© 1997 John Knox Press

2012 paperback edition
Originally published in hardback in the United States
by John Knox Press in 1997
Louisville, Kentucky

12 13 14 15 16 17 18 19 20 21—10 9 8 7 6 5 4 3 2

Library of Congress Cataloging-in-Publication Data

Long, Thomas G.
    Hebrews / Thomas G. Long.
        p.   cm.—(Interpretation, a Bible commentary for teaching and
preaching)
    Includes bibliographical references.
    ISBN: 0-8042-3133-8 (alk. paper)
    1. Bible. N.T. Hebrews—Commentaries.   I. Title.   II. Series.
    BS2775.3.L66   1997
    227'.8707—dc21
                                                            96-49258

ISBN: 978-0-664-23873-5 (paper edition)

For Kim

SERIES PREFACE

This series of commentaries offers an interpretation of the books of the Bible. It is designed to meet the need of students, teachers, ministers, and priests for a contemporary expository commentary. These volumes will not replace the historical critical commentary or homiletical aids to preaching. The purpose of this series is rather to provide a third kind of resource, a commentary which presents the integrated result of historical and theological work with the biblical text.

An interpretation in the full sense of the term involves a text, an interpreter, and someone for whom the interpretation is made. Here, the text is what stands written in the Bible in its full identity as literature from the time of "the prophets and apostles," the literature which is read to inform, inspire, and guide the life of faith. The interpreters are scholars who seek to create an interpretation which is both faithful to the text and useful to the church. The series is written for those who teach, preach, and study the Bible in the community of faith.

The comment generally takes the form of expository essays. It is planned and written in the light of the needs and questions which arise in the use of the Bible as Holy Scripture. The insights and results of contemporary scholarly research are used for the sake of the exposition. The commentators write as exegetes and theologians. The task which they undertake is both to deal with what the texts say and to discern their meaning for faith and life. The exposition is the unified work of one interpreter.

The text on which the comment is based is the Revised Standard Version of the Bible and, since its appearance, the New Revised Standard Version. The general availability of these translations makes the printing of a text in the commentary unnecessary. The commentators have also had other current versions in view as they worked and refer to their readings where it is helpful. The text is divided into sections appropriate to the particular book; comment deals with passages as a whole, rather than proceeding word by word, or verse by verse.

Writers have planned their volumes in light of the requirements set by the exposition of the book assigned to them. Biblical books differ in character, content, and arrangement. They also differ in the way they have been and are used in the liturgy, thought, and devotion of the church. The distinctiveness and use of particular books have been taken into account in decisions about the approach, emphasis, and use of space in the commentaries. The goal has been to allow writers to develop the format which provides for the best presentation of their interpretation.

The result, writers and editors hope, is a commentary which both explains and applies, an interpretation which deals with both the meaning and the significance of biblical texts. Each commentary reflects, of course, the writer's own approach and perception of the church and world. It could and should not be otherwise. Every interpretation of any kind is individual in that sense; it is one reading of the text. But all who work at the interpretation of Scripture in the church need the help and stimulation of a colleague's reading and understanding of the text. If these volumes serve and encourage interpretation in that way, their preparation and publication will realize their purpose.

The Editors

ACKNOWLEDGMENTS

This commentary is deeply indebted to the work of many specialists in the study of Hebrews, whom I have gotten to know and admire through their commentaries and scholarly monographs. In particular, I owe much to Harold W. Attridge, William L. Lane, Paul Ellingworth, R. McL. Wilson, and L. D. Hurst.

Attridge's superb volume in the Hermeneia series is the Mount Everest of commentaries on Hebrews—hard to climb, but the view from the top is magnificent. As for Lane, every time I ventured out in the light of day onto one of those rocky patches of land, which abound in Hebrews, I would find that Bill Lane had been out there since before dawn working faithfully and leaving not even the smallest stone unturned.

Ellingworth is the rare commentator on Hebrews who combines a good grip on the text with a keen sense of humor. He begins his own commentary by telling the story of the congregation of university students who were being treated in chapel to a longish reading of that section of Hebrews that twists and turns through a labyrinthine discussion of the significance of Melchizedek. When the lector came to the verse that begins, "What makes this still clearer . . . " (7:15), the congregation, Ellingworth reports with a wink, burst into spontaneous laughter.

Wilson has the uncanny knack of saying things plainly and of giving clear and reasonable answers to the kind of questions people really ask about Hebrews. Hurst brings not only the gift of careful and able scholarship to the study of Hebrews, but also the added virtues of levelheadedness and sanity. Like the book of Revelation, Hebrews is a symbol-rich, complex text, and it can be a tribal campground for cultists, tending to attract more than its fair share of symbolic speculation, hermeneutical bank shots, and downright weird interpretations. Hurst does the heroic service of sifting through the conjectures, wild and otherwise, and making good sense about the theology of this enigmatic document.

I also want to thank six very fine colleagues. Three of them—Eun Joo Kim, Carol Antablin Miles, and Stephen J. Quinlan—when they were doctoral students slogged through the text of Hebrews with me; as the Preacher of Hebrews himself might put it, they "were tested by what they suffered." The other three—Paul Achtemeier, Patrick D. Miller, and James L. Mays, editors of this Interpretation series—were most supportive and patient beyond measure. Again to echo the Preacher's words, they "endured to the end." I am indebted to all of these colleagues, since whatever strengths this commentary has are due in no small measure to their efforts.

It has been a wonderful privilege and a support to my own faith to explore this magnificent text. To the friends and colleagues who took me by the hand and guided me along the path—those named here and many others unnamed—I am profoundly grateful.

Thomas G. Long

Princeton Theological Seminary

CONTENTS

INTERPRETATION

Introduction

Among the books of the New Testament, the epistle to the Hebrews stands out as both strange and fascinating. Unique in style and content, as a piece of literature it is simply unlike any of the other epistles. Though some of its phrases are among the best-known and most often quoted passages in the New Testament, many contemporary Christians are largely unacquainted with the book as a whole, finding themselves lost in its serpentine passageways and elaborate theological arguments.

For those who take ropes and spikes and torches and descend into the murky cave of Hebrews, there is much about this document we wish we could discover, but our historical lanterns are too dim. For example, we wish we knew who wrote this curious epistle. Even though many names have been suggested—Apollos, Barnabas, Luke, Clement of Rome, Priscilla, and Silvanus, to mention a few—the arguments are not strong for any candidate. We actually have a firmer grasp of who did *not* write Hebrews than who did, since on stylistic grounds alone, it is a virtual certainty that the apostle Paul did not pen this letter. But who did? The best answer to that question is the comment of Origen in the third century: "But who wrote the epistle, in truth God knows."

We also wish we knew more than we do about the recipients, the first readers. Were they in Rome? Jerusalem? Colossae? Were they Gentiles? Jews? A mixture? We can only guess at the answers to these questions. The one current geographical reference in the book, which mentions Italy, is ambiguous (see comment on 13:24). Early on, someone attached a title to this document—"To the Hebrews"—but whoever did that was probably just speculating about its original recipients and was as much in the dark as we are.

Moreover, we would like to be able to pinpoint the date of Hebrews, but we can only provide an approximate range. Clement of Rome appears to quote Hebrews in a letter written sometime near the end of the first century, so it had to be composed before then. Also, most scholars believe that the elaborate christology of Hebrews could not have developed overnight and would more likely reflect the theological activity of the second or third generation of Christians. Putting these thoughts and a few other bits and pieces of evidence together, most scholars make an educated guess of A.D. 60 to 100 as the possible span during which Hebrews was composed.

So we peer into the depths of the text unsure of who wrote it, to whom, from where, or when. Imagine being handed a book today with the comment, "Here, you may enjoy this. It was written in America or Russia or France, I'm not sure, by a Jew—or was it a Gentile?—anyway, it was written sometime between 1920 and 1970. Enjoy." As Luke Johnson has observed, "Like its own description of Melchizedek (7:3), Hebrews appears in the canon 'without father or mother or genealogy' . . ." (Johnson, p. 412).

But even though we cannot know everything we wish we knew about Hebrews, there is still much that can be seen and learned by dwelling in the text itself, by exploring its contours and accepting its own internal structures and constraints.

First, when we read through Hebrews and compare it to other literature of its day, it becomes clear that what we call the Letter to the Hebrews is not, in fact, a letter at all, at least not in the customary sense. Even though it has some epistle-like flourishes at the end (see 13:22–25), the main body of Hebrews bears all the marks of an early Christian *sermon*, what the author calls a "word of exhortation" (13:22), a homily of the sort surely preached in many of the first Christian congregations. Early Christian sermons were heavily influenced by the style of preaching done in the synagogue, and in terms of structure and methods of biblical interpretation, Hebrews appears to be an example of a sermon that is rabbinical in design, Christian in content, and heroic in length.

What about the Preacher? It is probable (though not absolutely certain) that the author of this sermon was male (a self-reference in Hebrews 11:32 is masculine; thus, for the sake of convenience, we will refer to this commentary to the writer as the "Preacher" and as "he"). He had significant command of the Bible (which was, for him, the Septuagint), classical rhetoric, and the Greek language (the Greek of Hebrews has often been called the best in the New Testament). What is more, though the basic framework of his thought is Jewish, he also employed neo-Platonic philosophical categories. In short, the Preacher gives every evidence of being a quite well-educated Jewish Christian with broad training in Hellenistic thought.

2

There are a few other shards of evidence about the Preacher. He knows a Timothy (13:23), and if this is the Timothy who shows up elsewhere in the New Testament, which is probable, this puts our Preacher in the Pauline world of missionary activity. Also, the Preacher sends this sermon to a congregation he knows—he in fact is part of the community—and, though he is separated from them for the time being, he plans to return soon (13:19, 23). It may be that he was, like Paul, one of the traveling preachers who moved around the ancient world engaging in missionary activity.

The Preacher is not preaching into a vacuum; he is addressing a real and urgent pastoral problem, one that seems astonishingly contemporary. His congregation is exhausted. They are tired—tired of serving the world, tired of worship, tired of Christian education, tired of being peculiar and whispered about in society, tired of the spiritual struggle, tired of trying to keep their prayer life going, tired even of Jesus. Their hands droop and their knees are weak (12:12), attendance is down at church (10:25), and they are losing confidence. The threat to this congregation is not that they are charging off in the wrong direction; they do not have enough energy to charge off anywhere. The threat here is that, worn down and worn out, they will drop their end of the rope and drift away. Tired of walking the walk, many of them are considering taking a walk, leaving the community and falling away from the faith.

We recognize the problem, of course, but the Preacher's response may astound us. What is most striking about Hebrews is that the Preacher, faced with the pastoral problem of spiritual weariness, is bold enough, maybe even brash enough, to think that christology and preaching are the answers. The Preacher does not appeal to improved group dynamics, conflict management techniques, reorganization of the mission structures, or snappy worship services. Rather, he preaches—preaches to the congregation in complex theological terms about the nature and meaning of Jesus Christ.

This Preacher does not float around on the surface where the desires of people cluster eagerly around this or that fad; he dives to the depths, to the hidden places where profound symbols work on the religious imagination to generate surprise, wonder, gratitude, and finally obedience. As strategies go, the Preacher's approach to ministry is so out of phase, so counter-intuitive, so in violation of the notion that congregations are allergic to serious theological thinking, that it probably should be seen as refreshing, and maybe even revolutionary.

3

Jesus, the Last Word, and the First

HEBREWS 1:1–4

The book of Hebrews begins not just with a thought, but with a sound, the sound of a preacher's voice. When the first phrase of Hebrews is read aloud in the original Greek, we can hear with the ear what could easily be missed with the eye alone: the richness of its tones and the rise and fall of its melody. The rhythms and resonances of the words leap off the page. From the very opening sentence, then, the reader of Hebrews is aware that, though what follows is filled with profound theological concepts and symbols, this is not a lecture or an essay or a philosophical treatise; this has the unmistakable sound of a *sermon*.

It is almost as if the Preacher who composed Hebrews spreads out sermon notes on a pulpit somewhere, looks out at the congregation, pauses a moment in dramatic suspense, and then begins with words as graceful and rhythmical as the beat of a human heart: *"Polymeros kai polytropos palai . . . "* ("In many fragments and in many fashions in former times . . . ," 1:1). Like the initial line of Lincoln's Gettysburg Address, "Fourscore and seven years ago . . . ," these opening words of Hebrews display the cadence, the alliteration, and the keen awareness of the musical flow of beautifully spoken language that signal a carefully and poetically crafted oral event, a style that is sustained throughout the book. In black and white on the printed page, Hebrews appears to be a bit like an epistle, or even a theological monograph, but, when it sounds in the ear, we know immediately that we are not in the library reading an essay but in the pew listening to a sermon.

The eloquence of Hebrews is so striking that, over the years, many have conjectured it must have been written by Apollos, a well-known early Christian preacher, described in Acts as "an eloquent man" who "spoke with burning passion" (Acts 18:24–25). No one today knows, of course, who wrote Hebrews (see Introduction), but one can certainly see why Apollos's name would appear high on the list of possibilities.

4

Whoever wrote Hebrews was indeed "eloquent" and "burning with passion."

Even if we cannot solve the mystery of who wrote Hebrews, we do wonder about this author's purpose in producing such an odd hybrid: a written document crafted to sound like a sermon. Hebrews possesses an especially strong oral, sermonic quality because it was designed actually to be read aloud as a part of congregational worship, and the writer, an insightful and gifted preacher, did what effective preachers customarily do: employed language in ways that would have aural impact when spoken aloud to a group gathered for worship. In other words, there is a possibility that Hebrews is a sermon manuscript that a preacher in one location wrote for another preacher to preach in some other place. But even if this is not the case, even if Hebrews is not written literally to be read in a service of worship in the sanctuary, it *is* written for an act of worship in the imagination. No matter where or when Hebrews is read, even when it is read silently and alone, it transports us into the sanctuary, to the place of praise and to the occasion of the sermon. Its metered measures evoke the ethos of worship and the familiar tempo of proclamation, and this is theologically significant in at least three ways:

1. *The Evocative Text.* Like every effective sermon, even those that make hard and demanding challenges, Hebrews is crafted to be savored and enjoyed, not simply devoured and endured. There is evocative pleasure in reading and hearing this well-spoken text. From the outset, the readers (and hearers) recognize the rhythms of a fine sermon and set their expectations accordingly. "Faith comes," writes Paul, "from what is heard" (Rom. 10:17), and the writer of Hebrews would emphatically agree (see 2:1, 3).

In the gloomiest days of the Great Depression, President Franklin Delano Roosevelt spoke this strangely lovely and memorable phrase: "The only thing we have to fear is fear itself." These were not simply historic words *about* courage, they were words that generated courage. Hearing them did not merely convey information about being confident in the face of fear; hearing them evoked that very confidence, created a world where that boldness could be possible. In curious way, then, Roosevelt's phrase can be called "pleasurable," since it transports the hearer from a constricted and frightening world to a place of promise and hope. Just so, the "hair-raising eloquence" of Hebrews, its surprising and breathtaking rhetorical hills and valleys, the shapely and pleasurable contours of its speech, are no mere ornaments; they create a landscape on which the gospel can be seen in the vividness of its many colors, seen against the gray backdrop of all lesser alternatives,

5

and, having been seen, can become a joyful, confident, and life-giving event of faith for the readers.

2. *The Communal Text.* The "oral tone" of Hebrews recreates the communal, congregational event of hearing, as opposed to the individualized act of reading. A student of the spoken word, Walter Ong, observes that "the spoken word forms human beings into close-knit groups. When a speaker is addressing an audience, the members of the audience normally become a unity, with themselves and with the speaker." But if the speaker decides to clarify a point by asking the audience to refer to a handout, the result is that each person "enters into his or her own private reading world, the unity of the audience is shattered, to be reestablished only when oral speech begins again" (Ong, p. 74).

The Preacher of Hebrews has produced a written sermon, but one with the marks of an oral event. As such, he does not address discrete individuals, but rather "brothers and sisters, holy partners in a heavenly calling" (3:1).

3. *The Dialogical Text.* Hebrews, like all good sermons, is a dialogical event in a monological format. The Preacher does not hurl information and arguments at the readers as if they were targets. Rather, Hebrews is written to create a conversation, to evoke participation, to prod the faithful memories of the readers. Beginning with the first sentence, "us" and "we" language abounds. Also, the Preacher employs rhetorical questions to awaken the voice of the listener (see 1:5 and 1:14, for example); raps on the pulpit a bit when the going gets sluggish (5:11); occasionally restates the main point to insure that even the inattentive and drowsy are on board (see 8:1); doesn't bother to "footnote" sources the hearers already know quite well (see the familiar preacher's phrase in 2:6: "Someone has said somewhere ... "); and keeps making explicit verbal contact with the listeners (see 3:12 and 6:9, for example) to remind them that they are not only supposed to be listening to this sermon, they are also expected, by their active hearing, to be a part of creating it. As soon as we experience the rise and fall of the opening words of Hebrews, the readers become aware that they are not simply watching a roller coaster hurtle along the rhetorical tracks; they are in the lead car. In Hebrews, the gospel is not merely an idea submitted for intellectual consideration; it is a life-embracing demand that summons to action.

So as an evocative, communal, and dialogical text, Hebrews is not a tight argument, hard as a diamond with sharply cut facets; it is, instead, a sermonic exhortation (13:22) with an open weave, porous to the participation of the readers. It finally stands or falls not on its irreducible logic but on its capacity to be the soil in which an event of faith grows in the imaginations of those who read it. The reader does not come to

6

the end of Hebrews exclaiming, "Q.E.D.; that proves it!" but rather, "Amen! I hear this, I see this in the eye of faith, I believe this, I will live this!" When faith sounds in the ear, then it reverberates in the heart.

God Talk (1:1)

In terms of theological content, Hebrews opens with a poetic description of divine revelation as the speech act of God (1:1). God is pictured not as a silent and distant force, impassively regulating the universe, but as a talker, as One who has been speaking, arguing, pleading, wooing, commanding, telling stories, conversing, and generally spinning words across the lines between heaven and earth since the beginning of time.

The concept of divine revelation as speech is, of course, a metaphor, but a crucial one. Primarily it implies that, just as speech is an active interruption of silence, a disturbance of the stillness caused by the force of sound waves, so revelation is an active intrusion by God into our world and not a passive process. God moves the powers; God causes the sun to rise, God shakes the foundations; God breaks the chains; God labors in the world: all of the activity of God in creation reveals the character of God and is gathered up in the concept of divine revelatory speech.

In this sense, revelation is far more than mere human discernment of the holy; it is an event, an act of God toward humanity. Revelation is being "spoken to"; it is a holy summons, a disturbance of our peace. Revelation is not initially what we do to find and to name God, but what God does towards us to seek and to save and to restore all creation. Revelation is not human beings bringing ourselves to the place where we can see God hidden in every flower, star, and cloud, but God bringing us to the awareness that the heavens are preaching a word we could not know on our own and that flowers, stars, clouds—indeed the whole universe, as well as the entire fabric of human history—are telling a story of God's glory beyond our imagining. Revelation is not primarily the discovery of some grand design stealthily concealed in the complex patterns of nature, awaiting a science sophisticated enough to map it, but a shout in the street crying news we could not have anticipated, news that God is at work in creation, providing and saving, reconciling and judging, nurturing and healing. God *speaks.*

Every talker needs a partner, someone to listen and to speak in return, and God's conversational confidants have been, in particular, "our ancestors" (1:1, Greek = "fathers"), that is, the people of Israel, the Old Testament people of God. There is a reciprocal relationship implied between the speech of God and the people of God. The recipients of the divine word are God's people, but it is by virtue of

7

being addressed by God, gathered up in the holy conversation, that they are made God's people in the first place. In short, God turned toward the Hebrews and "talked them into being" the people of God, the children of the promise (see 6:13–15). The speech of God creates its own family of faithful hearers: "ancestors," not in the biological sense, but in the acoustic sense, a genealogy of those who have been hearers of the Word and thus kinfolk in the faith. The writer of Hebrews, faithful to the narratives of the Old Testament, knows that to be the people of God is not primarily to be given secret illumination or mystical enlightenment, but rather to be drawn into a lively and life-changing conversation. This God is One who speaks eventfully, and the people of God are those who have ears to hear and who speak and act in response.

God speaks, Hebrews tells us, "in many and various ways" (1:1), which is more accurately rendered "in many fragments and in many fashions." Though some have argued that "fragments" and "fashions" are synonymous terms and that the writer is simply being redundant for rhetorical effect, the two expressions probably point to somewhat differing aspects of the experience of God's revelation:

1. God speaks "in many fragments," that is, a word here and there, now and then. The speech of God is not unbroken chatter, like an all-night radio talk show, but episodes of speech punctuating seasons of silence. God spoke, for example, to Samuel in the temple, but this event of divine speech interrupted a long stretch when "the word of the Lord was rare . . . " (1 Sam. 3:1). Or again, when the Canaanite woman came to Jesus, begging for mercy for her tormented daughter, his word of grace and healing came only after a cryptic period of silence (see Matt. 15:21–28, esp. v. 23).

In W. H. Auden's poem "Victor, a Ballad," Victor has been betrayed by his wife, and in his distress he flees his home on a desperate journey of grief. He walks out onto High Street, past the garbage dump, and out to the town's edge. There he stands in his sorrow, weeping.

> Victor looked up at the sunset
>   As he stood there all alone;
> Cried: "Are you in Heaven, Father?"
>   But the sky said "Address not known."
>   (Auden, *Collected Poems*, p. 140)

We do not know why the revelation of God is episodic, why God speaks in fragments, why the will of God seems crystal clear in one circumstance only to be an opaque "address not known" in another. We only know that there is a mysterious rhythm to the speech and silence

8

of God that uncoils from the wild and wise freedom of God and that it is the experience of faithful people to say, like the psalmist, "For God alone my soul waits in silence" (Ps. 62:1).

And it is also the experience of God's people that out of the silence God does speak, and speak in timely, healing, and strengthening ways. In *Bearing the Cross*, David Garrow tells about such a moment in the life of Martin Luther King Jr. In the middle of the Montgomery bus boycott, King was facing a personal crisis of confidence. With negotiations with the city bogging down and resistance from the white community strengthening, King was growing not only weary but frightened as well. He had received over forty telephone calls threatening his life and the well-being of his family. Late one night, King returned home from a meeting only to receive yet another call warning him to leave town soon if he wanted to stay alive.

Unable to sleep after this disturbing threat, he sat at the kitchen table and worried. In the midst of his anxiety something told him that he could no longer call on anyone for help but God. So he prayed, confessing his weakness and his loss of courage. "At that moment," he said later, "I could hear an inner voice saying to me 'Martin Luther, stand up for righteousness. Stand up for justice. Stand up for the truth. And lo, I will be with you, even until the end of the world.' " It was, realized King, the voice of Jesus speaking a word of promise, a word of reassurance, a timely word of comfort and strength (Garrow, p. 58).

2. God also speaks "in many fashions." The metaphor of divine *speech* encompasses, of course, the infinite ways that God's presence, activity, and will are made known to human beings. Sometimes God speaks through visions and by stimulating flashes of insight, at other times God speaks through political movements and the shaking of the powers. Here God speaks in a dream or a waterfall, there in a prophetic oracle or a pillar of fire, or again in the still small voice, the commandments of the law, the stories of kings, the restless and brooding Spirit at the heart of the creation, or the journey of the sun across the noonday sky. God speaks in the quietness of prayer and the noise of honest debate. God sometimes speaks in powerful moments of spiritual wonder and also in the seeming humdrum of committee meetings. God's speech can be heard when nations make peace and when neighbors speak kindness across the backyard fence. God speaks through the Bible and also through the touch of a caring hand at bedside. God speaks in the voices of the choir, the beauty of art, the spangling of the heavens with stars, and the cries of the hungry for food, the lonely for companionship, the sick for healing, the pressed down for hope. God speaks in "many fashions."

God's speech is almost always mediated speech. When God wants to talk to human beings, someone or something—a burning bush, or an angel, or the heavens, or a Moses, or a Jeremiah—is summoned to do the talking on God's behalf. According to the Preacher of Hebrews, the main way that God spoke to our ancestors was "by the prophets" (1:1). This may simply be shorthand for "in the Scriptures," but the phrase more likely refers not to the written texts of the Old Testament but to the *people* described there whose human words and activity became the vehicle of divine speech and disclosure: Moses, Aaron, Rahab, Deborah, Isaiah, Jeremiah, Amos, to name only a few.

A New Word (1:2a)

So with a single powerful opening phrase, the Preacher of Hebrews has summoned the majesty and pageantry of the whole Old Testament witness to God. "Long ago God spoke," the Preacher begins, and the imaginations of the readers are vibrant with memories of the mighty speech acts of God. God spoke the creation into existence and declared it "very good." God spoke to Abraham, summoning him from his father's house and promising to make him a great nation. God called Moses to be the liberator of God's people, and God spoke the law on Sinai. Through Isaiah and Ezekiel, Amos and Joel, Hosea and Jeremiah, God spoke, nurturing and disciplining, provoking and redeeming the people Israel. "Long ago God spoke to our ancestors. . . ."

Suddenly, however, the Preacher halts in mid-sentence, then, after a suspenseful pause, utters a startling word: "*but*. . . ." But what? Every sermon listener knows that the little conjunction "but" is a dagger, swiftly attacking whatever stands before in favor of what is about to come, a trumpet heralding the appearance of something unprecedented. The word "but" is a rhetorical clue that what the Preacher has just been saying, indeed what the hearers have been taking in without question, is about to fall under challenge. Something new is about to emerge to rival the old, and the language of contrast forms a familiar biblical pattern. "*But* now thus says the Lord, . . . I am about to do a new thing" (Isa. 43:1,19) "You have heard it said . . . *but* I say unto you" (Matt. 5:21, 22).

"Long ago God spoke to our ancestors . . . by the prophets, *but* . . ." The words are a flare across the night sky signaling that now a fresh form of divine speech has broken across human hearing. God has "in these last days . . . spoken to us by a Son" (1:2), who is, of course, Jesus.

The argument is building toward the crucial contrast that will serve as a main theme of much of Hebrews, specifically the distinction between the ways that God spoke to former generations, and the definitive, climactic, and decisive word that, "in these last days," God has spoken through Jesus. Frederick Buechner playfully points to one aspect of this contrast (*Wishful Thinking,* p. 97):

> God never seems to weary of trying to get himself across. Word after word he tries in search of the right word. When the Creation itself doesn't seem to say it right—sun, moon, stars, all of it—he tries flesh and blood.
>
> He tried saying it in Noah, but Noah was a drinking man. . . . He tried saying it in Moses, but Moses himself was trying too hard; tried David, but David was too pretty for his own good. Toward the end of his rope, God tried saying it in John the Baptist with his locusts and honey and hell-fire preaching, and you get the feeling that John might almost have worked except that he lacked something small but crucial like a sense of the ridiculous or a balanced diet.
>
> So, he tried once more. Jesus as the mot juste of God.

What God has "spoken" in the Son is both continuous and discontinuous with the Old Testament narratives of divine disclosure. This interplay is expressed in the ambiguous phrase "in these last days" (2:1), which is something of a double entendre. Taken one way, this phrase connotes "at last" or "finally" and, as such, implies that God who spoke in many fragments and in many forms in the past has now, *at last,* spoken the definitive word. The emphasis here falls on continuity with all of the other words spoken by God to Israel; every prior word spoken by God to the people of God has been leading up to this final, consummate word. The word spoken in Jesus the Son is, in the theology of Hebrews, the last and perfect pearl in a beautiful strand of divine words.

Taken another way, however, the phrase "in these last days" should be read as an eschatological phrase, namely with the import that the Son is a word unlike any previous word, a word spoken to God's people from the end of all time into the middle of time—from God's future into the historical present. The emphasis here falls on the discontinuity of this event of revelation, on the fact that God's word in Jesus marks a decisive turning point in the ages. The Son is the breaking in of God's victorious reign, a word announcing the dawn of the triumph of God that rings down the curtain on the grinding cycles of history. The word spoken in Jesus is not simply an elaboration of what God has already done and said; there is something new here, something trail-blazing, something superior.

11

EXCURSUS:

Hebrews and Judaism

Hebrews's opening contrast between the speech of God "long ago" and the new word "spoken to us by a Son" raises an important theological question that will reappear at various points in the epistle: Is the message of Hebrews essentially anti-Jewish? Because the Preacher of Hebrews speaks of the Old Testament law as "weak and ineffectual" (7:18), of the old covenant as "obsolete" (8:13), and of Jesus as having a "more excellent ministry" and as "the mediator of a better covenant . . . enacted through better promises" (8:6), it is tempting to read Hebrews in sharp, triumphalistic "Christianity-is-superior-to-Judaism" terms.

To read Hebrews exclusively this way, however, is to blur some subtle distinctions and finally to distort the relationship between old and new in the epistle. We cannot pretend, of course, that Hebrews is somehow theologically neutral or that it does not possess a lofty and commanding christology. Hebrews unapologetically intends to magnify the power and the meaning of what God is saying and doing in Jesus Christ and to strengthen the readers' confidence in their Christian confession of faith. On the other hand, it is crucial to remember the Preacher's conviction that the God who speaks in Jesus is the very same God who spoke to "our ancestors in many and various ways," the same God who spoke to Abraham and Sarah, to Moses and Miriam, to Deborah and Jeremiah. God's speech did not suddenly change its essential character when it came to Jesus but was always the "good news" of blessing and peace across the generations (see 4:1–2). But if the God who speaks through Jesus is the very same God who spoke through Moses and the prophets, then how can the Preacher of Hebrews speak of the word disclosed in Jesus as "better" and "more excellent" without somehow denigrating God's earlier words?

First, it is important to keep the rhetorical situation of Hebrews in mind. The original readers were not students in a class on world religions debating the relative merits of Judaism versus Christianity. They were disheartened members of a Christian community who had begun to lose their grip on their own beliefs and commitments. The Preacher responds to them as any good pastor would, by reassuring them that holding fast to their faith is truly the best way. This reassurance is more than mere cheerleading, however; it was based on the

12

Preacher's own conviction that the promises of God made in Jesus are worthy of trust, indeed that holding fast to those promises is a "more excellent" way.

Second, when the whole of Hebrews is taken into account, we can see that the Preacher understands the word spoken "in these last days . . . by a Son" as a superior word in two ways, neither of which casts away or undermines God's prior revelation. The first way that the word spoken "by a Son" is superior is by virtue of being the last and ultimate word in a great sequence of divine words. Imagine a great chasm between God on the one side and suffering and broken humanity on the other that must be bridged if human beings are to be rescued and creation brought to its consummation. In order to span the gap, God engages in a series of saving acts, redemptive "words," that are forged together like links on a great chain stretched across the divide. God calls Abraham to leave his ancestral lands, stirs up the midwives Shiphrah and Puah to civil disobedience, summons Moses to liberating leadership, enrolls Isaiah through a moment of liturgical mystery—each of these divine actions, and many others, forming saving links that are joined to the growing chain of redemption. Jesus is the final link in this chain, the one that at last accomplishes the connection. Each link in the chain is valuable and, indeed, necessary, but without Jesus the chain will not reach. It is the final link, the last word spoken by a Son, that completes the chain and fits it for its saving purpose.

The second way that the word spoken "by a Son" is a superior word is that Jesus is more than just the last link in the chain of redemption; Jesus is the culmination of divine revelation, "the perfecter of our faith." In order to understand what this may mean, consider another analogy. Suppose that a young woman has just graduated with honors from Harvard. Adding to the pride of this occasion is the fact that she is the only member of her family ever to attend college. However, as she reflects on what made this day possible, she is aware that everything about her heritage has, in a sense, been pointing toward this accomplishment. For example, her great-grandfather, who could neither read nor speak English, immigrated to America to find freedom for himself and a more hopeful life for his children. One of her grandfathers was a tailor who, though he could not afford to provide a college education for his children, nevertheless instilled in them a love of learning and an intellectual curiosity. Her mother encouraged her to have the boldness to apply to Harvard, worked in a bakery to help pay the costs, and prayed for her every day.

Now this young woman's graduation from Harvard is the culmination,

13

the fulfillment of generations of striving and working, hoping and trusting. Without diminishing the dreams, the sacrifices, the prayers, and the
yearnings of those who went before her, it can be said that she has carried her family's heritage to a new and more excellent level. Indeed, all
that has gone before her has come to flower in this achievement; she has
brought her family legacy to fulfillment, or to use the language of Hebrews, to "perfection."

So the promises of God spoken through Abraham and Sarah and
Moses and Miriam and Isaac and Rebekah and all of the others whose
stories constitute the narrative fabric of the "old covenant" anticipate
the final word spoken in Jesus and are brought into laser-sharp focus
in the disclosure of the Son. The word spoken in Jesus does not void
the previous promises of God; it fuses, clarifies, and fulfills them; it
brings them "to perfection."

Christ for the World We Sing (1:2b–4)

The very mention of the Son in 1:2 leads the writer of Hebrews
into a lyrical moment. He begins to sing, or, as some scholars have suggested, to quote a hymn in good preacherly fashion. The rest of this in-
troductory section (vv. 2b–4) is probably derived from an early Christian hymn known by heart to the first readers, and it consists almost
entirely of a series of doxological phrases naming the praiseworthy
characteristics of Jesus. As the Preacher intones the familiar choruses,
he is surely confident that the hearers will respond with the refrain. Indeed, reading this section of Hebrews is much like hearing a preacher,
his voice rising with excitement, suddenly break into a verse of "All
Hail the Power of Jesus' Name," and to have the congregation join in,
"Let angels prostrate fall; bring forth the royal diadem, and crown him
Lord of all."

Specifically, Jesus is described in the following ways:

a. As the "heir of all things, through whom he created the worlds"
(1:2). This phrase is like a tuning fork. As soon as it is struck, a multi-
tude of Old Testament allusions begins to vibrate in response. In the
Old Testament, God's people are described as heirs of "the land" (see
Deut. 12:9, 19:10), and certain key persons (for example the "servant"
of Isa. 53:12 and the apocalyptic king of Dan. 7:14) are promised a rich
inheritance. Psalm 2:8, the most direct allusion in the Hebrews text,
presents "the nations" as the inheritance of God's son. Hebrews
weaves all of these threads together and augments them by naming
the Son as their heir, not merely of the land or of the nations, but of
"all things."

14

The irony is that the Son, who is heir of all things, also created all things. Jesus, who is the "last word," is also the "first word." The writer of Hebrews here connects Jesus to the figure of Wisdom, who was understood to be the inventive hand of God in fashioning the creation (see Prov. 8:22–31; Wisd. Sol. 7:22). The idea of the Son creating his own inheritance eventually grows into highly developed doctrines of the preexistence of Christ. Here, though, it may best be seen in a less precise sense, as an awestruck liturgical affirmation that Christ is all in all, at the beginning of time and at the end of it; that "all things have been created through him and for him" (Col. 1:16).

The idea that Jesus is the heir of all things addresses the human need to know where life is ultimately headed. Does the one who ends up with the most toys, or the most troops, really win? Does history flicker out with a whimper? Do the rich keep on getting richer and do the violent always bear it away, world without end, amen? The Preacher of Hebrews assures his congregation that, when all is said and done, life does not belong to the demagogue, the oppressor, the tyrant, or the warrior; it belongs to Jesus Christ. The creation does not disintegrate in violence, chaos, and futility; it endures at a holy inheritance. Human beings do not end up in meaninglessness; they end up as the treasure of the beloved Son.

b. As "the reflection of God's glory and the exact imprint of God's very being" (1:3). Here, again, the writer of Hebrews draws upon the wisdom traditions (see esp. Wisd. Sol. 7:26) to affirm the clarity and value of what has been seen and heard in Jesus. Jesus, as the Son, is not an approximation of divine truth; in him the very nature of God shines forth brightly. Jesus is not *a* word from God; he is *the* divine word. To paraphrase Paul, in former times God's people may have "seen through a glass darkly," but, in Jesus, we see God "face-to-face."

There was once a man from a small southern town whose father died when the man was an infant. While other boys would work in the fields or play catch or go fishing with their fathers, this man had no father, not even any memories. As he grew older, he became obsessed by the need to know something, anything, about his father. Whenever he met a person who may have known his father—a schoolteacher in the town where his father had grown up, a retired minister who once served in his father's home church, an aging cousin of his father—he would urgently ask, "What can you tell me about my father?" He spent a lifetime piecing together shards of recollection, pieces of anecdotes, trying to get a picture of the man who was his father.

15

In a much deeper sense, the Preacher knows we all hunger to know God the Father. We are on a desperate search for information about our heritage, intimate knowledge of the one who gave us birth. All spiritual quests are, in their own ways, attempts to ask, "What can you tell me about my father? What do you know? What do you remember?" The answer of Hebrews is that, when we have seen the Son, we have seen the Father. Or as Calvin put it, "The Father, however infinite, becomes finite in the Son. . . . He shows himself only in the Son—as though he says, 'Here I am. Contemplate me.'"

c. As the one who "sustains things by his powerful word" (1:3) and who "made purification for sins" (1:3). Here the Son, who at the beginning was the agent of creation and who at the end inherits all things, is portrayed as at work in the flow of human history, holding things together and, by a definite act (the cross, though it is not here named directly), having renewed the brokenness of creation.

d. As seated "at the right hand of the Majesty on high" (1:3). This is a clear allusion to Psalm 110:1, a favorite text of early Christians (see Hay, *Glory at the Right Hand*) and a key psalm for the author of Hebrews (see 1:13; 8:1; 10:12; 12:2). If the previous phrase about "purification of sins" referred to the death of Jesus, this phrase refers, in a single image, to the resurrection and exaltation of Christ.

e. As "superior to angels" (1:4). This phrase is both a fitting and customary conclusion to the doxology and a transition to the rest of the material in this chapter. Like the Christ hymn of Philippians 2:5–11, Hebrews 1:1–4 has traced the christological parabola (see the discussion of the "parabola of salvation" in comments on 1:5–14), following the trajectory of the divine Son from creation sweeping downward to the cross and up to the heavenly place of majesty, where the Son is exalted with "a name above every name," even the names of the angels. Now that the Preacher has arrived at the theological climax of this section of the sermon—the affirmation that the Son is higher even than the angels—he now amplifies this with a rhetorical flourish in the verses that follow.

Jesus Was No Angel

HEBREWS 1:5–14

The rest of chapter 1 (vv. 5–14) consists of a constellation of seven quotations from the Old Testament, mainly from Psalms, all in service of elaborating at great length the point the Preacher has just made in verse 4: Jesus, the Son, is "much superior to the angels."

The Preacher's Question (1:5)

The section begins with a good preacher's device, a rhetorical question: "For to which of the angels did God every say, 'You are my Son; today I have begotten you?' " (1:5). The implied answer, of course, if that God never said anything like this to any angel, but only to Jesus the Son. The quotation itself is a verse from Psalm 2:7, which refers to the special relationship in Israel between the king and God, but its original context in the psalm is not nearly so important as the fact that this verse, with its image of God bringing alive ("begetting") a Son, had become a standard scriptural quotation in early Christian preaching to refer to the baptism of Jesus (see Matt. 3:17; Mark 1:11; Luke 3:22) and especially to the resurrection (see, for example, Acts 13:33). In other words, the Preacher is saying, "You know that God raised the beloved Son Jesus from the dead. Have you ever heard about God doing this for any angel?"

A second sonship quotation is added for emphasis: "I will be his Father and he will be my Son" (from 2 Sam. 7:14 = 1 Chron. 17:13). Again, for the Preacher's purposes the historical context of this verse pales before its use as a stock reference in early Christian preaching, where it was employed to point to the spiritual familial relationship between God and Christian believers (see 2 Cor. 6:18 and Rev. 21:7) and, in an intensified way, to the unique bond between God and Jesus.

Fleeting Angels, Eternal Son (1:6–12)

Now that the Preacher has evoked what God did *not* say about angels, in 1:6–7 he turns to two Old Testament references to report what God *did* say about them. First God said, "Let all God's angels worship

17

him," that is, worship Jesus the Son, a quotation derived from the Septuagint version of Deuteronomy 32:43 or perhaps from Psalm 97:7. The point is clear: angels are the worshipers, Jesus the one adored. The timing of this worship is uncertain, since the Preacher says ambiguously that the angels were commanded to worship the Son "when [God] brings the firstborn into the world" (1:6). Does this phrase refer to the incarnation, when God brought Jesus (the "firstborn," see Rom. 8:29; Col. 1:15; Rev. 1:5) into the world of human history, or to the ascension, when the victorious Jesus was welcomed in splendor by the heavenly court, or perhaps to the parousia, when the coming of the Son in power and glory will be trumpeted by the angels (see Matt. 24:30–31)? The Preacher's meaning is elusive, but the time reference is not the crucial issue; the emphasis here falls on the claim that the angels bow down before the Son, not on the question of when.

The second quotation about the actions of angels is from Psalm 104:4. The Hebrew text of this verse, as reflected in the NRSV translation, pictures God turning the natural elements into obedient servants: "You make the winds your messengers, fire and flame your ministers." The Preacher, however, quotes not the Hebrew text but the Septuagint, which reverses the subjects and predicates: "He makes his angels [messengers] winds and his servants flames of fire" (1:7). When the verse is turned around this way, the point seems to be that angels are servants of God, subordinate in status, and that they are fleeting and transitory. Like the wind, they exert force but then vaporize; like flames, they burn with power but then flicker out.

By contrast to angels, who are subordinate in status and fleeting by nature, the Son is majestic and everlasting. To score this point, the Preacher recites another pair of Old Testament quotations applied christologically (1:8–12). The first of these, Psalm 45:6–7 (cited in 1:8–9), was originally a psalm for a royal wedding in Israel, but it had probably become a standard christological reference in the liturgy of the early church (see Lane, *Hebrews 1—8*, p. 29). In any case, it appears in Hebrews as one of the few places in the New Testament where Jesus is explicitly addressed as God: "Your throne, O God, is forever." The Preacher is not making a systematic argument about the divinity of Jesus, however, but claiming that, unlike the angels, Jesus' reign is eternal and exalted above all others ("beyond your companions").

The second quotation, from Psalm 102:25–27 (cited in 1:10–12), refers to Jesus as "Lord" and creator ("the heavens are the work of your hands") and reinforces the idea implied in the first quotation that Jesus' status, in contrast to the angels, is eternal ("they will perish, but you remain . . . they will be changed, but you are the same").

18

The Preacher's Question
Revisited (1:13–14)

In 1:13, this section of the sermon moves toward its zenith. Good pulpiteer that he is, the Preacher signals the approaching climax by coming full circle to the rhetorical question with which he began "But to which of the angels did God ever say . . . ?" The Preacher has woven a patchwork quilt of Old Testament quotations into a hymn of praise to Jesus the Son, who is superior to all angels. Now this doxology moves to its crescendo as the Preacher intones Psalm 110:1, "Sit at my right hand until I make your enemies a footstool for your feet."

The readers would recognize this beloved verse immediately since it was a favorite in the preaching and liturgy of the early church (see Mark 12:36; Acts 2:34–35; Eph. 1:20–22; Col. 3:1; Heb. 10:12–13; 1 Peter 3:22). Indeed, when Hebrews was originally read aloud to the congregation, the hearers would probably have joined in and finished the quotation with the lector. Understood christologically, the reference conveys that Jesus' work of redemption is done. Jesus has triumphed over evil and death on the cross. "The strife is o'er, the battle done; the victory of life is won." Now he is seated in the place of authority, at the right hand of God, and all that remains is for God to make a "footstool" out of his enemies, in order to bring to completion the redemptive work that the Son has set into inevitable motion. The Preacher's voice rises to a peak to nail down his point: No one has ever said that about an angel, who are but servants "in the divine service, sent to serve" those whom the Son has redeemed (1:14).

For ten verses, the Preacher has been singing about the superiority of the Son to the angels. Why? What's the problem? Many commentators have been somewhat confounded by this section, basically wondering why the Preacher is making all the fuss. Two matters are particularly perplexing. First, the Preacher seems, quite frankly, very long-winded here, running on excessively about a relatively minor and perhaps tangential theological contest: Jesus versus the angels. Why does the Preacher spend so much energy and space, not to mention a basketful of scriptural quotations, on a technical theological issue that turns out to be of little importance in the total flow of the argument of Hebrews?

In the second place, the use of the Old Testament here seems to be, to put it mildly, a tad arbitrary, especially when judged (as commentators tend to do) by the standards of contemporary biblical scholarship. What is particularly bothersome is the author's tactic of lining up what

19

amounts to a string of Old Testament "proof texts," jackhammered out of their contexts. The Preacher seems so eager to make his point, to show that the Old Testament supports his christological view that Jesus is higher than the angels, that, as one commentator's observes, he "simply quotes what appears to suit his purposes" (Wilson, p. 37).

The perplexity clears somewhat, though, when we look more closely at what the author is trying to achieve in this extended and exegetically venturesome section. What is the problem here? One frequent suggestion about why the author waxes at such length here about Jesus' superiority to the angels is that the first readers of Hebrews must have been theologically confused about angels and desperately in need of being straightened out doctrinally. Some have speculated that the congregation engaged in outright angel worship, while others have proposed a less drastic source of mischief, perhaps a vague notion of angels as the mediators of worship or maybe a foggy christology that mixed up the work of Christ with the functions of angels.

Such proposals are not outside the range, since doctrinal problems about angels seem to have occurred elsewhere in the early church, and, in fact, Col. 2:18 may constitute an attack on such beliefs and practices. However, a major obstacle to the idea that an angel heresy is afoot is the fact that, once we leave this section of epistle, the issue of angels is basically dropped. If a faulty angel theology was the major peril to the congregation, one serious enough to merit a treatment of this length at the beginning of the sermon, we would expect the matter to reappear, especially given the Preacher's tendency to revisit his major motifs. But any hint of an angelic threat disappears after chapter 1, and in fact angels are viewed quite positively in the few fleeting references that occur elsewhere (see 12:22 and 13:2).

So if an angel heresy is not the concern, what has the Preacher so wrought up here? It is far more likely that the real issue for the first readers of Hebrews is not a problem with angels—but a problem with *Jesus*. The underlying issue being addressed in this section, indeed a crucial matter throughout the whole of Hebrews, is not that the readers find too much glory in angels but that they find too little of it in Jesus.

Evidently the first readers of Hebrews were undergoing some sort of distress (see, for example, 12:3–13), and, as a consequence, they were having difficulty holding on to their faith. They were weary and disheartened. All they could feel was exhaustion; all they could see was trouble. As for Jesus, he appeared to be of precious little help or comfort because all the naked eye could see of him was the bloodied, bowed, humiliated teacher from Nazareth who suffered and shouted in pain on a cross and who seemed to be unable to save himself, much less anybody else. Surely Jesus shared their suffering, but sharing suffering is not the same thing as transforming it. The problem with Jesus was that he was too human, too vulnerable. The objection to Jesus was that he appeared to be less than God, indeed he even seemed "lower than the angels," dragged down to the depths of human weakness where he was powerless to help.

In short, the first readers of Hebrews were tired of being Christians, tired even of Jesus. The response of the Preacher to their discouragement is not to pretend that their experiences are not painful or that their vision is blurred. He does not pat them on the head saying, "There, there, things are not so bad," nor does he dispense superficial advice to "look on the bright side," or "count your blessings." The Preacher knows that their suffering is authentic, the threats around them real. What the Preacher does instead is to *preach* the truth of the gospel that lies beyond sight and touch. He reminds them that the deepest and most trustworthy reality cannot be seen by the naked eye; it can only be *heard.*

True, judging by what the eye could see, Jesus was broken, shamed, and defeated by the powers of the world. But the whole truth about Jesus is not visible to the eye, and the Preacher's main theme is that the hope and steadfastness of the congregation depends upon their ability to pay more attention to what is *heard* than to what is seen (2:1). They must hold fast to what is *confessed* by the mouth (4:14), must study the *oracles* of God (5:12), must trust what God has now *spoken* by a Son (1:2). The Preacher is now telling them that their tangible experience is not the whole story, evoking in their hearing what they could not see with their eyes, reminding them in speech of what they know not by touch or sight but by faith birthed in the ear: that Jesus the Son, who was experienced as weak and beneath the angels, was "made lower than the angels" by God in order to save broken humanity; that this bloodied and bowed Jesus who died in anguish on the cross is the heir of all things, seated in power at the right hand of the most high, and "as much superior to angels as the name he has inherited is more excellent than theirs" (1:4).

So the whole book of Hebrews can be understood as a sermon addressing this need, but it is not an entirely new sermon. Instead, the Preacher rings the changes on an old favorite, a familiar early Christian sermon pattern that could well be called "the parabola of salvation" sermon, a cherished design that Paul also employed in Phil. 2:5–11 (see comments above on 1:4).

The "parabola of salvation" sermon brings on a lofty pinnacle with the exalted Son, high above all things: "the reflection of God's glory and

21

the exact imprint of God's very being" (1:3). But then the trajectory sweeps downward into painful human experience and tragic history. The glorious Son, for the sake of redemption, is made "lower than the angels" and endures the shame of the cross (12:2). And then the curve arcs heavenward once again, sweeping up toward victory, as Jesus is raised from death and, holding fast to those he has redeemed, takes his triumphant seat "at the right hand of the throne of God" (12:2).

Here is a graphic representation of the "parabola of salvation" sermon, which also depicts the basic underlying structure of the Preacher's christology:

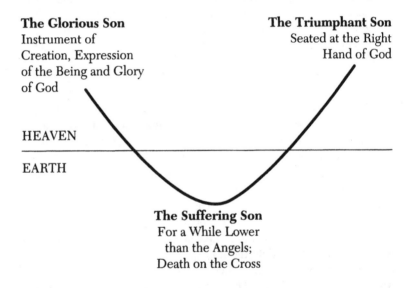

The Glorious Son
Instrument of
Creation, Expression
of the Being and Glory
of God

The Triumphant Son
Seated at the Right
Hand of God

HEAVEN

EARTH

The Suffering Son
For a While Lower
than the Angels;
Death on the Cross

Figure 1

The weary congregation of Hebrews longed for a gospel without a cross, a redemption without sacrifice, a faith without pain—something pristine and holy, something that does not exhaust the faithful with calls to put one foot in front of the other in daily obedience, something beautiful like an image of God in an unspoiled heaven surrounded by lovely angels singing untroubled hymns. Anything but a weeping, suffering Jesus marching through tragic history with his head bowed and his face bloodied.

But the Preacher will not compromise the gospel, will not reduce it to the power of positive thinking. As the chapters of Hebrews unfold, the Preacher will leave his heavenly starting point and follow the parabola to the depths of the cross and to the daily sacrifices of the Christian life. But here in the opening chapter he sustains the sense of the glorious heights before he descends to the abyss. He knows that the gospel gains its power when the hearers are able to hold in their faithful imaginations the central paradox of the faith: the Jesus who was made "for a little while lower than the angels" was, is, and always will be the Son exalted above all things, "superior to the angels." The Jesus who suffered a humiliating death at the hand of evil is the same Son who is "the reflection of God's glory." The "heir of all things through whom God created the worlds" is the very one who, for our salvation, became one who had nowhere to lay his head and "endured the shame" of the cross.

So as he gets ready to plunge to the depths the Preacher wants his hearers to hold the image of the exalted Son even as they move to the cross. Thus he prolongs the thrilling view from the top of the parabola by doing what preachers have always done to engender and sustain ecstacy: he sings a doxology, quoting songs of praise his congregation knows well. Like a contemporary preacher on a homiletical roll quoting stanzas of "Jesus Shall Reign Where'er the Sun," the Preacher quotes verse after verse of familiar Scripture, each citation heightening the emotional level of the message. In their worship and instruction, early Christians regularly employed collections of Old Testament scriptures applied to Christ, and the Preacher's citations were almost surely drawn from such a set of scriptures his hearers had said and sung many times in praise of Christ. As theologian William Placher maintains,

> Christian reading of the Bible, then, takes Christ as a clue to the shape of the whole of scripture. We see the "character traits" exemplified in Jesus in the way other parts of the Bible describe God at work—even, albeit more tentatively, in the work of God throughout the one world in which we live and move and have our being—and these stories thus begin to shape the way we live our lives. (Placher, p. 342)

Thus, the Preacher is not "proof texting"; he is making what they already know and believe alive in their hearing.

Hearing Testimony in a Higher Court

HEBREWS 2:1–4

Ethics Class:
Danger Ahead (2:1)

Chapter 1 ended on a sustained crescendo, the Preacher pulling out all the rhetorical stops to sing praises to the eternal and exalted Son. Like an Olympic diver poised on the high board, the Preacher has allowed the suspense to build before the inevitable plunge, which the congregation knows must surely come. Having heard the "parabola of salvation" sermon many times before (see comments on 1:5–14), the congregation is aware that the christological doxology on the lofty heights must be followed by a swift descent to the depths of the cross.

Curiously, though, just as the congregation expects the Preacher to spring from the board, he pauses to give them a lesson in ethics. In 2:1–4, the christological hymn-sing is suspended in favor of instruction about the Christian life, a practical, homiletically sophisticated, ethical challenge to be attentive, steadfast, alert, and obedient to the faith. As such, it represents the first of several segments of ethical material woven into the doctrinal fabric of the sermon, and it displays the vital connection between theology and ethics in Hebrews (see "Excursus: What's the Big Idea in Hebrews . . . ?" below, p. 31).

The Preacher, who has been directing the gaze of the congregation toward heaven and the exalted Son, abruptly redirects their vision away from heaven and toward earthly matters. He has been urging them to look up in order to see the exalted Son; now the Preacher exhorts them to look around, toward the character of their own lives, toward the danger of their "drifting away" (2:1). The organ and the choir have been thundering a doxology of the exalted Lord in chapter 1, but

24

suddenly "All Hail the Power of Jesus' Name" gives way to "Take Time to Be Holy." Ethics class begins, and the Preacher issues sharp and direct warnings for the pilgrim people. No wonder one commentator has called this section an ethical "salvo" and a "parenetic interlude" (Attridge, p. 63).

On closer inspection, though, what could seem to be an interruption in the flow of the sermon turns out to be a crucial and transformative segment. This ethical section is no detour; it is a flashing yellow light on the main highway, a warning about the perils that lie directly ahead in the sermon. The sermon will soon enter into dangerous territory—the narrative of the incarnation, the story of Jesus' anguish and vulnerability—and a warning is necessary for this risky journey. Beginning with 2:5, the Preacher will take the congregation by the hand and lead them down the treacherous road that Jesus traveled, the pioneer trail of suffering and death. Like a tour guide preparing to take a group through a threatening part of town, telling them to hold on to their wallets and purses, the Preacher pauses at the top of the street and warns the congregation to hold fast to their confession of faith. "Tell me the stories of Jesus, I love to hear," we glibly sing, but the author of Hebrews knows that it can be a dangerous thing to tell the Jesus story. Ironically, the reciting of the Jesus story not only can strengthen faith, it can also imperil faith. Therefore, the Preacher warns, stay together, listen carefully, and hold onto your creed.

What is so dangerous about the Jesus story? What is at risk in a discussion of the incarnation? The peril lies in the fact that the incarnation, taken out of context, is a discouraging story of bitter defeat. "We had hoped," say the two disheartened followers on the Emmaus road, "that he was the one to redeem Israel" (Luke 24:21). Only the tragic dimension of the Christ event is visible on the screen; the cosmic meaning of the cross is obscured from view. Taken by itself, the story of Jesus is a mournful story of a victim overpowered by his enemies. Taken alone, the narrative of Jesus from birth to the cross is the moving but finally despairing story of one who courageously took on the powers that be but, in the end, was no match for them.

We easily forget that the central narrative of the Christian faith is, on the face of it, a deep embarrassment. Often we have turned the passion story into harmless sentiment and the cross into a piece of costume jewelry, losing touch with what early Christians painfully knew, that Jesus died in shame (12:2) and that the cross is, to rea-

25

sonable eyes, an inexplicable foolishness and a stumbling block to faith.

No wonder the Preacher had taken such pains earlier to contrast the Son to angels, to emphasize that, when the full truth is known, Jesus the Son is higher than the angels (1:5–14). On paper, angels are sweet, attractive, and brightly lit, something like the Easter Bunny, while the Jesus who walked up Calvary's hill is a bloodied embarrassment, a serious deterrent to upbeat religion and "the power of positive thinking." After all, no one ever spat on an angel or drove a crown of twisted thorns into an angel's brow. No angel ever hung on a cross, an object of derision to passersby. No one ever mocked an angel: "He saved others; he cannot save himself." No angel ever cried out in the anguish of death, "My God, my God, why have you forsaken me." Unlike Jesus, angels do not share human flesh and blood, and thus no angel's blood is ever spilt and no angel's flesh is ever torn by spikes.

The question to be faced by the writer of Hebrews, the question that evidently threatened the first readers of Hebrews (and perhaps threatens contemporary Christians as well), is this: If Jesus is truly the Christ, then what is the meaning and purpose of his suffering? Or more to the point, what earthly good is a suffering Christ? The psychologist M. Scott Peck begins one of his best-selling books with a truth everyone knows: "Life is difficult." Anyone who has ever fought an addiction, wept over a troubled child, discovered a malignancy, cried out for justice, wondered where to find enough food to make it through another day, faced the end of a loving relationship, spent a cold night sleeping under a freeway bridge, coped with a disability, or stood in grief at a graveside knows that life is a demanding, fevered struggle. Even people who seem peaceful and carefree on the surface are often fighting tough battles every day. We are all keenly aware that "the days of our life are . . . toil and trouble" (Ps. 90:10), and that all human striving ends in the embrace of the feared enemy, death. So the question is, What is different, worthy, or redemptive about the life of Jesus, which to all appearances was also brief, full of pain, and consumed at the end by death? Yes, he shared our humanity, but did not Jesus' humanity ultimately defeat him as it defeats us, too?

We can best understand the response of the Preacher by reminding ourselves of the theological shape of the sermon he is preaching, the "parabola of salvation," which we first encountered in chapter 1 (see figure 1, p. 22, and comments on 1:5–14):

26

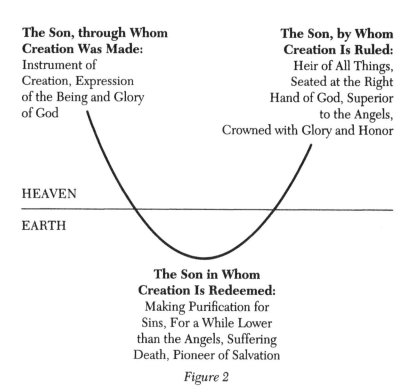

**The Son, through Whom
Creation Was Made:**
Instrument of
Creation, Expression
of the Being and Glory
of God

**The Son, by Whom
Creation Is Ruled:**
Heir of All Things,
Seated at the Right
Hand of God, Superior
to the Angels,
Crowned with Glory and Honor

HEAVEN

EARTH

**The Son in Whom
Creation Is Redeemed:**
Making Purification for
Sins, For a While Lower
than the Angels, Suffering
Death, Pioneer of Salvation

Figure 2

Note that there is a border, a dividing line between heaven and earth. Above the line, the Son is exalted. Below the line, the Son suffers and dies. Above the line, the Son sits at the right hand of God in majesty; below the line the Son walks down the lonely road of human suffering and rejection and hangs on a cross in shame.

We live, of course, below the line, in human history. Above the line is that which transcends history, that which was true before time existed, will be true after time will have ceased, and even now is true. It is important to note that what is above the line cannot be seen. It is hidden from sight, and it is this hiddenness that constitutes the danger to hope, the threat to steadfast faith. In terms of immediate experience, human beings can see only those realities below the line. We can see the suffering; it is the victory we cannot see. We can walk down the corridors of hospitals and nursing homes, through the streets of cities, and across battlefields, and we can see, smell, and touch the suffering. It is the hope we cannot see.

27

Just so, the suffering and dying Jesus was visible to the whole world, and, as an observable moment in the tragic unfolding of human history, his cross seems to be just another moment of torture in a long line of crosses dragged up an endless chain of Calvarys. The story of his life of suffering sounds like just one more chapter in the sad, unending narrative of human oppression. In the broken, pain-soaked march of human history, the death of Jesus is plain to see—and, frankly, not all that unusual. Innocent people suffer and die all the time. Jesus was a good man who fell victim to the cruelties and the indifference of the world. There are stories like his in the newspaper every day.

Everyone can see the shame of Jesus' death; what we cannot see is how Jesus' death brings life. What is hidden is that, through Jesus' suffering and death, God "will wipe every tear from their eyes" and that "death will be no more; mourning and crying and pain will be no more" (Rev. 21:4). This is beyond the range of the eye, but *not*—and this, as we have noted, is the Preacher's key point—beyond the range of the ear. We cannot *see* the world being created and restored through the Son, but we can *hear* it. We cannot *see* the victorious Son seated at the right hand of God while all his enemies—oppression, hatred, deceit, and death—are placed under his feet, but we can *hear* this word. In worship and confession; in the mouths of preachers, teachers, prophets, and other witnesses; in all places where the gospel takes on the sound of faithful human talk, the very speech of God breaks forth in human speech, and, like a clarion sounding through thick fog, pierces the gloom to announce the presence of what we can surely trust though we cannot yet see it: that though "we are being killed all day long . . . we are more than conquerors through him who loved us," for nothing "in all creation will be able to separate us from the love of God in Christ Jesus our Lord" (Rom. 8:36–39).

That we can hear this word, and through hearing it believe what we cannot see, is a crucial claim for the Preacher of Hebrews and the reason why the section on ethics appears at this point in the sermon. Through the membrane separating heaven from earth, God speaks, and the Preacher issues an ethical call to attentiveness and obedience, summoning the congregation to perk up their ears and to "pay greater attention to what we have *heard* so that we do not drift away from it" (2:1).

The Preacher as
Defense Attorney (2:2–4)

28

The Preacher has a problem. He wants to issue a call to ethical responsibility. He wants the congregation to live the Christian life, holding fast to their confession of faith but, as every good preacher knows, it is useless simply to say to a congregation: "Behave yourself. Live your faith." It does not help even to be pious and say, "*God* wants you to behave yourself." The problem is not knowledge; the hearers know what their moral obligations are. The problem lies deeper, in the will. The acids of life have eaten away at their confidence; the grind of daily trouble has fatigued their faith. They know what the gospel is; they just do not trust it any longer. How can they go on believing what is preached when everything around them seems to deny it?

Since the experience of the congregation has evidently placed the gospel on trial and found it wanting, the preacher responds with a daring piece of rhetorical strategy. He files an appeal. Imaginatively painting the picture of a courtroom, the Preacher boldly strides in as an attorney with a new brief for the defense (2:2–4).

What does a good lawyer do? First, the applicable legal precedents must be cited. In this case, the pertinent precedent is the Old Testament law, the Torah, what "God spoke to our ancestors" (1:1). Since the question before the court is whether God's word "spoken to us by a Son" can be trusted, the lawyer challenges the court to examine God's track record. In the past, God spoke the Torah (which the Preacher calls "the message declared through angels" [2:2], reflecting a popular view that angels accompanied God at Sinai and, at the same time, linking this passage to the prior discussion about angels), and everyone concedes that this prior word, the law of God, was "valid" and trustworthy (2:2; "valid" is a technical legal term; see 9:17, where it is used to describe the point at which a will takes effect).

How do we know that the Old Testament law was valid? Because every time God's people failed to obey it, they paid the price and "received a just penalty" (2:2). The argument here is not that God's people are like cattle hemmed in by the electric fence of the divine law, and they know that the law is activated because every time they try to cross it they get a jolt of punishment. The argument, rather, is that God's law is like parental wisdom to children about what makes life good and whole. The proof of the validity of such wisdom is that when the children follow the parents' guidance, life is full of joy, but when they do not, their foolishness carries its own consequences and life becomes painful and tragic. Now if the old law was valid and true, argues the Preacher using the logic of the-lesser-to-the-greater, how much more is the new "law" of the gospel, the message of salvation in the Son, valid and true, and thus not to be neglected (2:3; see a similar statement in 12:25).

But a good lawyer does not stop with precedents; witnesses must be called as well. First, the Preacher calls Jesus himself, the first witness to the gospel, to the stand. The gospel "was declared at first

29

through the Lord" (2:3). Jesus "came to Galilee, proclaiming the good news of God" (Mark 1:14), and what he preached and taught was not merely *about* the work of God in the world; it was itself the living and active word, having authority beyond other teachers (Matt. 7:29).

Moreover, the witness of Jesus is corroborated by others, and the Preacher calls these witnesses to the stand as well. First, there are "those who heard him" (2:3). If the gospel came through the preaching and teaching of Jesus, there were those in earshot of his proclamation, followers of Jesus and firsthand hearers of the word, who have borne witness to what was said. The author clearly refers here to the apostles as the primary hearers of the gospel, but, as Lane has pointed out, the word "apostle" is not used here since Hebrews reserves that title for Jesus (3:1). "The highest office the writer acknowledges within the larger Christian community is that of 'a hearer.' . . . By speaking of 'the hearers' . . . all interest is concentrated on the message, not the office . . ." (Lane, *Hebrews 1—8*, p. 39).

In skillful lawyerly fashion, the most impressive witness is saved for last: God is called to the stand to bear witness to the validity of the gospel. God's testimony—consisting of signs, miracles, and manifestations of the Holy Spirit—powerfully confirms the gospel's authenticity. What is this divine testimony? It can be understood on two levels. On the first level, the author of Hebrews is referring to the miracles that were a part of the proclamation of Jesus and to the dramatic signs that resulted from the apostolic preaching of the gospel (see Luke 10:17; Rom. 15:19; 2 Cor. 12:12).

At a second level, however, the Preacher is talking in a more local way about the ongoing life of the Christian community, of the church. The author is reminding the readers about how Christian congregations receive the gospel and what evidence they have in their own life of its truthfulness. The gospel, first proclaimed by Jesus, comes through witnesses: preachers, teachers, parents, friends. It was reported that the theologian Karl Barth was once asked by a skeptical professor from East Germany, "How is it that such a learned, civilized, intelligent man like yourself can believe in something like the resurrection?" To which Barth is said to have replied, "Because, my friend, my mother told me."

But the gospel is not just a set of ideas; it is a way of living validated by manifestations of the Spirit. People are reconciled; forgiveness is experienced; the gifts of teaching, healing, discernment, wisdom, and prophecy are realized in the community; the Scriptures speak anew; the chains of oppression are broken. All of these gifts of God, received in their own worship, fellowship, and service, bear testimony to the trustworthiness of the gospel and serve to reassure the congregation that what they have heard is true and not mere whistling in the night.

EXCURSUS:
What's the Big Idea in Hebrews—Theology or Ethics?

Through the years, students of the book of Hebrews have been intrigued, and occasionally mystified, by the way the writer flows back and forth between highly doctrinal material and practical ethical instruction. One moment, the writer will sound like a philosophical theologian, a metaphysician, only to turn the next moment with the barest of transitions to concrete pastoral matters such as worship, marriage relations, hospitality, and charity. This frequent shifting between what the readers are called to believe and how they are called to live has led to a debate among scholars over the primary aim of the writer. Hebrews is obviously concerned about both doctrine and ethics, but which is foremost? Is the writer interested in proper doctrine essentially because it leads to an ethical life? Or is it the other way around? Does the author urge the ethical life because it leads to a deeper knowledge of God? In short, is Hebrews mainly a doctrinal sermon punctuated by ethical illustrations, or is it a practical sermon on Christian living buttressed with theological affirmations?

Attridge is surely heading in the right direction when he forbids us to choose between the two, insisting, rather, that Hebrews is "a balanced combination of doctrinal exposition and parenesis" and that an "assessment of its overall meaning needs to take both dimensions of the work equally into account" (Attridge, *Hebrews,* p. 21). However, "balance" is perhaps too timid a word to describe accurately the linkages between theology and ethics in Hebrews. Balance can imply merely a static relationship—equal portions of theology and ethics in motionless equilibrium. But the writer of Hebrews does not place theological material into a sealed container on one side of the scale and then carefully ladle matching portions of ethics into a similar sealed vessel on the other side. The relationship between theological knowledge and ethical practice, instead, is interactive and reciprocal, each growing out of, leading into, and profoundly affecting the other. Sound doctrine leads to solid ethics, and, conversely, living the Christian life leads to theological wisdom.

Hebrews is not alone, of course, among New Testament documents

31

in relating doctrine to practice, but what is unique about Hebrews—and what often makes it difficult to discern the living relationship between theology and ethical action—is the mode of theology that the Preacher of Hebrews believes is pertinent for Christian living. Hebrews's theological style is highly symbolic, philosophical, almost an "academic" manner of theological reflection. For the most part, the writer of Hebrews states theological views in an analytical, deeply considered, precisely stated fashion. So as a sermon Hebrews is not merely a practical guide for Christian living with a few theological tidbits tossed in for the ride. To the contrary, the Preacher of Hebrews beckons the hearers to put on their thinking caps and to enter into the strenuous world of primary theological analysis, where the biblical sources and the philosophical conceptual world of their time interact. What is more, the Preacher is bold enough to assert that all of this wrestling with weighty theological themes is crucial for the practice of the Christian faith in trying times; indeed, it is a matter of life or death.

In particular, Hebrews dares to suggest that getting clear about christology, as difficult and tangled as that doctrine is, actually leads to such virtues as steadfastness, hospitality, and hope—in short, the ability to "keep on keeping on" in the service of Christ. More surprising, perhaps, the writer of Hebrews appears also to be persuaded that the reverse is true as well, that walking the pilgrim way obediently and with faithful endurance clarifies one's christology, deepens theological wisdom, and increases the knowledge of God.

This refusal to drive a wedge between serious and sustained theology and serious and sustained ethics constitutes a significant challenge to our own time. In the relationship between theology and ethics, orthodoxy and orthopraxis, the tendency is to fall off on one side or the other. Today there are at least a few who would be content to define the Christian faith primarily in terms of cognitive belief in a set of profound ideas, master propositions arranged into a logical and coherent system. The relationship of God to humanity is thus understood primarily as a mental function: what we think of God and God's attitude toward us. The Christian life, therefore, consists mainly in getting one's theological thinking straight.

More prevalent, perhaps, is the contemporary view that thinking theologically is a leisure activity reserved for professional theologians and religious virtuosi. In this view, it doesn't much matter what theological ideas one believes to be true, so long as one is sincere. Theological reflection is a nicety for the seminary professor, the minister on "study leave," or the occasional super-religious layperson, but it can be

32

checked as excess baggage in the face of the crushing demands of the organizational church and the workaday life of the Christian. From this perspective, theological convictions are like parlor games, fun to talk about in discussion groups but finally of no consequence. One can hold rather loosely to this or that collection of theological thoughts, mix them up with other vague religious intuitions into a jumble of contradictory claims, or abandon them altogether, since what finally matters is not one's confession but one's conscience, not one's views but one's style of life. What one believes about God, the world, other people, and oneself is not nearly as important as the way one behaves, the kind of character one displays, as being a "good person," however that may be defined. "I'd rather see a sermon," goes the slogan, "than hear one any day."

For the author of Hebrews, however, it is not that simple. It is naive to think that one can sustain ethical action in a theological vacuum. If we do not have any coherent conviction about how God is restoring the broken creation and how our prayers and our efforts are incorporated into this divine action, if we do not know how working at a soup kitchen, or providing hospitality to the stranger, or laboring for criminal justice, or striving to serve the poor, or seeking human rights, or any other good work in this world fits into the larger theological picture of God's redemption, then we eventually lose heart, lose energy, and lose faith. The lines at the soup kitchen only grow longer; there are more strangers than we can care for and their needs overwhelm us; attempts to allow justice to take root find little sunshine and stingy soil; and the rich continue to get richer and the poor poorer. For all of our good intentions, we end up, like the original readers of Hebrews, with drooping hands and buckled knees and precious little hope for anything other than more of the same: "one damned thing after another."

That is why, then, that the author of Hebrews is urgent that "we must pay greater attention to what we have heard," to the word "spoken to us by a Son," to the theological whole of which our life and labor are but parts. By opening ourselves to what is spoken, to the proclamation of the gospel, we get what we need to face one more day with faith and hope. We discern how the fragments of our broken lives, the few seasons of our fragile pilgrimage, are gathered into the great parabola of God's victory sweeping through all time and space. Ironically, we also discover the reciprocal truth that somehow finding the theological energy to pick up the baton one more time and to stretch our weary legs for one more lap in "the race that is set before us" becomes itself a deep form of Christian knowing, a pathway to understanding God in Christ, whose way in the world is one of suffering.

33

Jesus: For A Little While Lower than the Angels

HEBREWS 2:5–9

Descending from the Heights (2:5–8a)

At the close of chapter 1, the Preacher rhythmically set forth a series of contrasts between Jesus and angels: angels are functionaries, but Jesus is a Son; angels are fleeting, but the Son is eternal; angels are servants, but the Son sits in glory at the right hand of God (see comments on 1:5–14). Now the Preacher sounds out one more distinction: at the end of time, the world-to-come will be subject to the authority of the Son, not to the angels (2:5).

At first this seems like simply one more item in the list, one more beat in the homiletical drum roll, but this last contrast actually signals a significant move in the sermon, a descent from the lofty peak of the Son's exaltation to the depths of the cross. The Preacher's anthem has been about the eternal Son, higher than the angels; now he will change to a minor key and sing of that time when the Son became "lower than the angels." The language of "subjection" (2:5), then, is a bit of sermonic wordplay. On the one hand, it continues the theme of the Son's glorious status, but on the other hand it makes a verbal link to a phrase in Psalm 8, and this gives the Preacher his new preaching text. Yes, Psalm 8 also uses the language of subjection (2:8), but not before it employs the phrase "lower than the angels" (2:7), and *that* is where the Preacher wishes to go.

So with Psalm 8 as his guide the Preacher will show that the subjection of the world-to-come occurs only after the Son, astonishingly, is made "lower than the angels," that is, made a full participant in the human condition. But this is a hard truth for the congregation to comprehend (see comments on 1:5–14 and 2:1–4). If, as the opening verses of Hebrews claim, the Son is the heir of all things, the reflection of God's glory, superior to the angels, and the Lord of all time, why did he walk the tragic road of human history to defeat and death? If Christ truly sustains all things by his powerful word, why do we see him weakly submitting to a cross of shame? The Preacher's christological treatment of Psalm 8 begins a detailed response to these questions, and this familiar Psalm is introduced to the congregation with the commonly used preacher's footnote "someone has said somewhere" (2:6).

Psalm 8 in its original Old Testament setting is about humanity in general. The psalm marvels that the majestic God, whose glory fills the skies, would nonetheless treat lowly human beings with great dignity. Literally translated, the psalm asks, "What is a man that you are mindful of him? What is a son of man that you watch over him?" and answers, "You have made him a little lower than the angels, crowned him with glory and honor, and set him over the works of your hands, subjecting all things under his feet."

But like many early Christian preachers, the Preacher of Hebrews treats the psalm as a statement not about all humanity but about one human being in particular: Jesus. According to the Gospel tradition, Jesus called himself the "Son of Man" (see Mark 2:10; Matt. 16:27–28), and it may be that this verbal coincidence encouraged a christological reading of the psalm (see Eph. 1:22; 1 Cor. 15:27). However, scholars disagree about whether the Preacher is drawing here on a fully developed "Son of Man" christological tradition, since that title and the associated imagery are lacking from the rest of Hebrews. Regardless of whether a refined "Son of Man" concept is in view, though, it is plain that the Preacher did see the psalm christologically, as a reflection of the cosmic journey of the Son from majesty through shame and back again to exaltation.

In this regard, it should be noted in passing that the NRSV translation of Hebrews 2:6–8 can be seriously misleading. In order to avoid gender-specific language, all masculine terms are made neutral and some singular nouns are made plural. Thus the NRSV renders "man" in the psalm as "human beings," "son of man" becomes "mortals," "him" is changed to "them," and "his" is translated "their." These otherwise laudable changes have the unfortunate side effect of obscuring the Preacher's christological application of the psalm, specifically that "man," "son of man," "him," and "his" are all treated as references to Jesus.

But if the NRSV translators have made changes in the psalm in the service of a prior theological conviction, they are in good company; so did the author of Hebrews before them. First, in order to make the psalm work even more effectively in his christological argument, the Preacher amended the original text. The portion of the psalm quoted by the Preacher states that God gave to humanity "dominion over the works of your hands" (Ps. 8:6), but the Preacher skips over that phrase (at least in the best attested manuscripts of Hebrews).

35

This omission is made probably because the psalmist is clearly talking about how God has made ordinary human beings managers and stewards over the world of nature, and that idea is confusing as a christological claim.

Second, the Preacher reverses the theological thrust of the original psalm. In its own setting, the psalm expresses astonishment over how high human beings are ranked on God's scale. Imagine, exclaims the psalmist, insignificant human beings are positioned just "a little lower than the angels" (Ps. 8:5). But the Preacher uses the psalm to voice amazement not over soaring heights but over surprising depths; the exalted Son, who towers over all time and space, was nonetheless willing to stoop to a status "lower than the angels," to join himself to the lowliness of the human condition.

There is one other translation issue of importance here. The original Hebrew text of Psalm 8:5 reads, "You have made him a little lower than the divine beings [angels]," but, as usual, the Preacher quotes the Greek Septuagint, not the Hebrew text. The Greek can be translated either "a little lower than the angels" (a statement about distance and rank) or "for a little while lower than the angels" (a measure of time). The NRSV wisely opts for the latter (*contra* the NIV), not only because it matches Hebrews 2:9 but also because the temporal rendering fits in with the thrust of the whole argument here. The Preacher does not wish to argue that Jesus was just a tiny bit lower than the angels in the hierarchy of creation, that he came just to the edge of human life and dipped his little toe into the pool of suffering. Rather, he wants to claim that, for a brief moment in time, the eternal and exalted Son purposefully and redemptively plummeted to the depths of human suffering and weakness.

Seeing Jesus,
Hearing the Gospel (2:8b–9)

By his use of the quotation from Psalm 8, the Preacher has now taken the full sweep of the event of Christ and grounded it in the Scriptures of the Old Testament. Before this point, the Preacher had quoted many Old Testament texts, each one supporting this or that claim about the Son, but here the Preacher has found a text he can unfold as a symbolic portrayal of the entire drama of redemption. Christologically applied, the psalm serves as a poetic and comprehensive illustration of what we have called "the parabola of salvation" (see comments on 1:5–14). It depicts the complete sweeping movement of the "Son of Man" from the eternal heights down through the angelic realms into the chasm of the human predicament and back up again into glory, where "God left nothing outside his control" (2:8).

More important, however, the psalm allows the Preacher to name a key and repeated theological theme of the entire sermon: the distinction between what we can see with our eyes and what we can see only by faith, "the assurance of things hoped for, the conviction of things not seen." The psalm's phrase about "subjecting all things under his feet" serves as the occasion for the Preacher to ring the joyful refrain, first intoned in 1:2, that the Son is the heir of all things and that God has placed everything in creation under his control (2:8a). But then, with great rhetorical finesse, he pauses and in effect turns toward the congregation with a lowered voice to say, "But on Monday morning it doesn't look that way, does it?" "As it is," he admits, "we do not yet see everything in subjection to him" (2:8b).

Every congregation knows well what the Preacher means. Look at the world around us, and it hardly seems that the Son of God is running the show. From the hole in the ozone to the torn fabric of society to the broken places in the human heart, all creation seems under the sway of tragic evil. The Preacher is telling the truth; far from being under the control of the victorious Son, the world looks chaotically out of control.

The Preacher's rhetorical skill is on vivid display here. He has slowed down the pace of the sermon and confided, to the sad assent of the congregation, that we do not yet see the victory of the Son. "What we *do* see . . . ," says the preacher, and then he pauses to allow the tension to build. "What we do see . . . ," and the congregation, who saw pain and trouble at every hand, surely began to fill in the blanks with their sorrow. "What we do see . . . ," and now the Preacher swiftly raises the curtain on the stage of human history. "What we do see is . . . *Jesus*" (2:9). In Greek the suspenseful effect is even more dramatic since the name Jesus is positioned at the very end of the long sentence, a technique for creating emphasis that the Preacher employs on all eight occasions when he uses the name "Jesus" (the others are 3:1; 6:20; 7:22; 10:19; 12:2; 12:24; 13:20; see Lane, *Hebrews 1—8*, pp. 48–49).

Now that the Preacher has placed Jesus firmly in view, he shuttles swiftly back and forth between what can be known about Jesus by sight and what can be known only by faith. In other words, the Preacher alternates between the truth about Jesus that can be *seen* and the truth about Jesus that must be *heard*. Everyone who saw Jesus arrested and tried and pushed around like a common criminal knows that he was "lower than the angels"; you could see that. But it takes hearing the word of the gospel to know that this same Jesus is "now crowned with glory and honor." Everyone who watched Jesus die in agony on the

37

cross knows about "the suffering of death"; that could be seen with the eyes. Only by what is heard through the ears, though, could it be known that this death was in order to save humanity, that "by the grace of God he might taste death for everyone" (2:9). This portion of the sermon is much like the word of the risen Jesus to the disheartened followers on the road to Emmaus (Luke 24:25): "Oh, how foolish you are, and how slow of heart to believe all that the prophets have declared! Was it not necessary that the Messiah should suffer these things and then enter into his glory?"

Several years ago, the White House correspondent for one of the major television networks prepared a report for the evening news on some aspect of Presidential politics. The words of the report, written and spoken by the correspondent, were basically critical and cast a negative light on the President's policies. However, the taped pictures that appeared on the screen to accompany the report were supplied by the White House from stock footage, and they showed the President in a series of flattering settings.

The day after the report was broadcast, the Director of the White House Office of Communications called the correspondent to compliment her on the report. "But why the praise?" she protested. "My report was critical of the President."

"Your words were critical," replied the official, "but you showed *my* pictures, and in the battle between the eye and the ear, the eye wins every time!"

No, says the Preacher, the eye does not win every time—not finally, not ultimately. The eye may win for "a little while," but when all is said and done, it is the gospel heard through the ear that turns out to hold the full truth. Yes, the Preacher says, Jesus did suffer. The whole world saw that. Yes, Jesus did exhibit the weakness of human flesh. Yes, Jesus did die, sharing the fate of all humanity. But those were only the pictures; listen to my words. Jesus was only "for a little while lower than the angels," and this descent into human history was for a distinct purpose. When one hears the full message of the gospel, one recognizes beyond mere sight that the season of Jesus' suffering was a necessary segment of the arc of grace that curves finally to the place we cannot yet see, to the place of triumph where the Son is even now crowned with glory and honor.

Pioneer and Priest

HEBREWS 2:10–18

In the previous section of the sermon, the Preacher proclaimed the gospel message that Jesus' suffering and death had a redemptive purpose. Everyone dies; all human beings "taste death" for themselves, but unlike ordinary mortals Jesus "tasted death for everyone" (2:9). How are we to understand this? How does the passion of Jesus connect to the suffering of all humanity?

It is to this complex question that the Preacher now turns, and we must thread our way carefully here because the Preacher, like many other preachers before and since, mixes his metaphors. Indeed, we have a collision and a collusion of images. Three major systems of images, not readily compatible, are employed to describe the Christ event, each laid upon the previous one like transparencies on an overhead projector.

1. *Hero.* The primary image, the one upon which the other two are overlaid, is the picture of Jesus as the mythic hero who descends into the world below, into the realm of death, to defeat the powers of death and to rescue those trapped in death's grip. This image, which is depicted in the "parabola of salvation" (see figure 2), was part of the common mythic machinery of the classical and Hellenistic thought worlds (see Attridge, pp. 79–82). It is in this context of rescuer that Jesus is called the "pioneer" of salvation (2:10), a rendition of a multifaceted Greek word that has also been translated as hero, champion, founder, author, guide, leader, and scout, among others. Some have even suggested that the description of Jesus as the "champion of . . . salvation" is a play upon a similar well-known description of the mythic hero Hercules, presenting Jesus, in other words, as "the new Hercules" (see Lane, *Hebrews 1—8*, pp. 56–57).

2. *Liberator.* Bolted to this mythic chassis is a second constellation of images, all growing out of a military metaphor of Jesus as the liberator. Like the allied troops who liberated Auschwitz, Dachau, and the other concentration camps, Jesus broke through the gates of death, destroyed the Commandant of Death (the devil), and liberated those imprisoned in fear (2:14–15). This "liberator" image does double duty,

39

since there are also hints here of the story of the Exodus and the liberation of the people of Israel from slavery.

3. *High Priest.* Finally, as a third metaphorical network juxtaposed onto the first two (and as something of a surprise), Jesus is described as a "merciful and faithful high priest" (2:17), who, like the High Priests of old, made "a sacrifice of atonement for the sins of the people" (2:17). Early in the sermon the Preacher had provided a slight foreshadowing of this imagery ("he had made purification for sins," 1:3), but the introduction here of the specific terminology of the high priest seems swift and unexpected.

Perhaps the image of Jesus as "high priest" was already familiar to the first readers of Hebrews and needed no elaborate introduction. It is more likely, however, that the Preacher has engineered a dramatic collision of images, evoking a gasp from the congregation as he suddenly draws together previously discrete images of Jesus: hero, liberator, and high priest. Like the turbulence created at the confluence of churning rivers, the merging of these disparate metaphors creates rippling undercurrents that capsize prior understandings and surge forth in unexpected directions. We can no longer simply think of Jesus as the "hero" without also remembering that he is also the "priest," and, moreover, Jesus the "high priest," presiding at the altar at the liturgical center of the universe, is at one and the same time the commando who broke through the barbed wire of the "death camp" of human pain, liberating the captives. Image piles upon image—the cosmic, the existential, and the liturgical—competing, conflicting, and complementing. The result of this churning convergence is that no longer can the grandest of human hopes for redemption be divorced from the bloody conflict with sin and death on the cross, and, likewise, no longer can the pain of human sin and suffering be seen apart from its sacramental connection to the priestly and atoning work of Christ.

This "high priest" image is crucial for the later development of the sermon, and it will reappear briefly in 3:1 and will form the central focus of an extensive discussion in 4:14—10:25.

The Pioneer Made Perfect (2:10)

The overall purpose of this passage, of course, is to explain how it was that the glorious Son of God was seen wearing a private's uniform and operating behind enemy lines; that is, to explain why it was necessary that Jesus, for a while, assumed a rank "lower than the angels," took on ordinary mortal flesh, and, as a consequence, suffered and died in combat with the forces of death.

The Preacher begins this explanation by saying that it was "fitting" that the Son should be a suffering pioneer, a bloodied hero (2:10). The term "fitting" is highly ironic, bordering on dark humor, since it is the language of etiquette and civility, something like Miss Manners deeming the placement of silverware to be "fitting and proper" or a psychologist meekly declaring someone's behavior to be "appropriate." The last thing a cultured Hellenist would call "fitting" is the notion of God being roughed up, sweltering in human pain. There are many possible reactions to the news that the "heir of all things," the Son who "sustains all things by his powerful word" was bullied around by a weak and vacillating Roman puppet and sent packing like a criminal up Golgotha to a brutal execution, but "fitting and proper" would not be among them.

The Preacher, however, has employed the term "fitting" in a specifically Christian way, clashing with the ordinary expectations of the term, in the same way that Jesus described his own baptism as "fitting and proper" over the objections of John the Baptist (see Matt. 3:13–15). Taken in the abstract, the idea of "God" is incompatible with the experience of suffering. What it means to be "divine" is to be "not human," to be defined by categories separate from the weakness, transience, and vulnerability that suffering entails. Thus any notion of "God" partaking of human suffering is inconceivable, sheer foolishness, hardly "fitting." Only in the light of the gospel narrative, only in the context of the story of the incarnation does the unthinkable become the necessary, the unimaginable become that which is "fitting," the incongruous become the indispensable, and the foolishness of the incarnate Son, crucified, dead, and buried, become the very wisdom of God.

Why was it "fitting" for the Son to suffer? Because it was through suffering that Jesus was made "perfect" (2:10); that is, suffering was the fitting way for Jesus to become "perfect." But in what sense did Jesus need to be perfected? The Preacher considers Jesus to have been "without sin" (4:15), so there is no idea here of an impure Jesus being morally perfected. Rather, the idea is that Jesus was made "fit" vocationally and functionally, not morally. The image is something like a machinist fabricating a part, fashioning it to fit perfectly and to perform its function. When the metal is shaped just right and the edges smoothed just so, the machinist can exclaim, "Perfect!" What is meant is the part not only fits just right, it will also perform its job to specifications.

It was through suffering, then, that Jesus was shaped and fashioned to perform his task in the drama of redemption. His purpose was to serve as the redeemer, the one who comes from God and rescues humanity from death. He is the mediator, the one who makes peace between a defiant humanity and God. These redeeming and mediating roles involve more than standing in the gap between God and humanity; they involve deep participation in both the life of God and the life of humanity. Through suffering, Jesus is made perfect in both directions.

In terms of participation in the life of God, suffering made Jesus perfect by testing his will to be obedient and faithful (2:18). In the book of Job, when God presented Job as an example of faithfulness, Satan challenged God by saying, "Skin for skin! All that people have they will give to save their lives. But stretch out your hand now and touch his bone and his flesh, and he will curse you to your face." In other words, "It is one thing to be faithful when somebody else suffers; it is another thing to be trusting and true when you, yourself, suffer." When Jesus suffered, he was the new and perfect Job, the one who remained trusting and obedient even in the midst of excruciating pain.

In terms of participation in human life, Jesus is made perfect in the sense that suffering joins him completely and empathetically to the human condition. Through his pain Jesus becomes a "brother" to every other human being, and this is a radical theological point. The Preacher is saying that when the gaze of the eternal Son of God encompasses a criminal on death row, when the glorified Son sees a homeless woman crawling into a cardboard box to keep from freezing in the night, when the Lord of all sees a man robbed of dignity and purpose by schizophrenia, when the divine heir of all things sees a mother weeping over the death of her child or a man battling the last savage assault of cancer or the swollen body of a child slowly starving to death, he does not see a charity case, a pitiful victim, or a hopeless cause. He sees a brother, he sees a sister, and he is not ashamed to call us his "brothers and sisters" (2:11). The Son of God does not wag his head at misery and cluck, "There but for the grace of God go I." Instead he says, "There because of the grace of God I am." As the psalmist puts it, "The Lord has compassion for those who fear him. For he knows how we were made; he remembers that we are dust" (Ps. 103:13–14). Because Jesus experienced rejection, pain, suffering, and death, his life is porous to the full range of human misery and oppression. By virtue of his passion, Jesus has compassion. Because he was himself "tested by what he suffered, he is able to help those who are being tested" (2:18). "God's love," states Hans Küng, "does not protect us *against* suffering, but it protects us *in* all suffering" (Küng, *On Being a Christian*, p. 436).

42

The Son Speaks:
Past, Present, and Future (2:11–18)

The Preacher emphasizes and elaborates the idea of Jesus' solidarity with the human condition by returning to a familiar pattern, "the parabola of salvation" (see figure 1, p. 22, figure 2, p. 27, and accompanying comments):

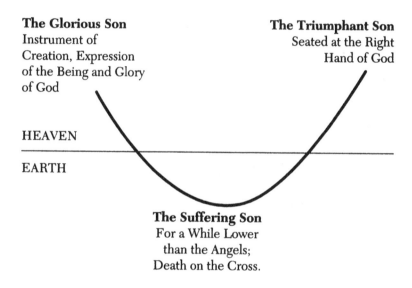

The Glorious Son
Instrument of
Creation, Expression
of the Being and Glory
of God

The Triumphant Son
Seated at the Right
Hand of God

HEAVEN

EARTH

The Suffering Son
For a While Lower
than the Angels;
Death on the Cross.

Figure 3

Here the "parabola of salvation" is traced by the citation of a sequence of three Old Testament texts, but they are not presented as Old Testament quotations. Rather, the Preacher imagines the Son himself speaking each one in turn, the first as "the glorious Son" prior to the incarnation, the second as the incarnate "suffering Son," and the third as the "triumphant Son" whose redemptive work is done. Taken as a set, then, these three quotations are arranged to show the parabolic journey of the pioneer of salvation.

The first citation, from Psalm 22:22, is couched in the future tense and expresses the intention of the Son prior to creation: "I will proclaim your name to my brothers and sisters . . . " (2:12). This implies the divine reason for the incarnation: the intention of the Son

43

to make the goodness of God known to human beings by becoming fully joined to humanity and by proclaiming the goodness and trustworthiness of God. The Son, reigning above all, was not content to remain aloof but chose to enter completely into human life. Interestingly, it is in Jesus' proclamation of the good news (and in the continued proclamation of that good news in congregational worship) that we see ourselves not only as Jesus' subjects, but also as his sisters and brothers.

The second quotation, "I will put my trust in him" (2:13), probably an adaptation of Isaiah 8:17, represents the trusting posture of the "Son in creation," bound to the human condition yet relying upon God even in the midst of persecution. The third quotation, from Isaiah 8:18, gives voice to the "Son victorious over creation," seated at the right hand of God and announcing the redemption of the faithful: "Here am I and the children God has given me" (2:13). By the work of the Son human beings, who toiled in fearful slavery to the powers of death, are now stationed in majesty as royal sons and daughters of God, joined to God through Christ. Thus these three quotations, lined up in salvation history chronology, constitute points along the parabola of God's gracious invasion of human history in Christ.

After providing the words of the Son through the three Old Testament quotations, the Preacher focuses the close-up lens on the second word, the middle period, the time of Jesus' being bound to the human condition. What, exactly, was Jesus doing when he cried out his confession, "I will put my trust in him?" The Preacher's answer: he was becoming a slave so that he could smuggle himself into the human slave camp.

Of the several views of the atonement found in the New Testament, here we see an image of Christ as the liberator, the one who breaks into the slave quarters and sets the slaves free. The Preacher pictures all humanity as slaves and the devil as the heartless slave master. Every slave master has a whip, a means of power and fear and control, and the devil's whip is death. All human beings are "held in slavery by the fear of death" (2:15).

The slave camp must be liberated from within, thus Jesus had to become a slave, had to come under the whip, had to submit himself to the power that makes of human life a toilsome servitude. He shared, then, what all the slaves share—flesh and blood and death (2:14)—so that as slave he could lead the uprising against the slave master.

44

As a slave, Jesus refused to obey the slave master. Instead, he obeyed the One who sent him, and trusted God to keep the promise.

He knew, of course, that his defiance would force the demonic slave driver to apply the whip of death, and he did. But the Son-become-a-slave never wavered. "I will put my trust in him," he said; "Father, into your hands I commend my spirit," he prayed, even as the last lash fell across his back.

When we see the Son of God not in the heavens or on a royal throne, but appearing in the slavequarters with whip marks on his back, then it is clear that he came to help us, "the descendants of Abraham," not the angels. Angels are not forced to work in the fields under the lash of death, but we are—and so Jesus became "like his brothers and sisters in every respect" (2:17). When asked what his credentials are for ordination to the high priesthood, he shows his scars as a sign of his mercy and faith.

In a sermon, George Ross once told of an event that occurred in England in the early days of the Salvation Army. A man with a charismatic personality and a magnetic speaking ability was traveling around the countryside presenting himself as Jesus Christ returned to earth. He claimed to heal the sick, to restore sight to the blind, and to perform other miracles, and he managed to gather an impressive following of believers and curiosity-seekers.

One evening he was lecturing in a great hall in London, when in the distance could be heard the sound of music, growing gradually louder and closer. A Salvation Army band was approaching the hall. Indeed, the little group of musicians entered the hall, tubas and trumpets blaring, and they marched right down the center aisle to the speaker's rostrum.

The Salvation Army captain motioned to the musicians, and the music ceased. Then he turned to the speaker and asked, "Are you really the Christ? Tell us plainly."

"Yes," replied the speaker. "I am the Christ returned to earth."

Looking at him steadily, the captain said, "Very well, then, show us your hands." At that point the band began to play again: "I shall know him, I shall know him, by the print of the nails in his hands!" (George Everett Ross, in Leonard Sweet, *Strong in the Broken Places*, pp. 39–40).

Jesus bears the scars of the cross, the scars of human suffering and death, and "he was tested by what he suffered" (2:18). For all of us who must still face suffering, for all of us who must still trudge to the cemetery in sorrow, we are not without comfort and help, for the great high priest who sits on the throne of glory has been there, too. He bears the scars of his testing, and he "is able to help those who are tested" (2:18).

45

House Church

HEBREWS 3:1–6

Holy Partners (3:1a)

In this passage, we once again observe a master preacher at work, this time employing a homiletical technique that could be termed "repetition and surprise." First comes the repetition. In 1:5–14, the Preacher's theme was the superiority of Jesus, in particular how Jesus was loftier even than the angels; now in 3:1–6 he appears to circle the runway by returning to this idea of Jesus' preeminence, this time in relation to Moses. "I have already proclaimed that Jesus is exalted, higher than the angels," the Preacher seems to say, "and now I want to make the case again, this time by showing that Jesus is greater than Moses, too." But just as the congregation is lulled into thinking that they have gotten the point, the Preacher springs a surprise. The congregation thinks that the emphasis is on the majesty of Jesus alone, but suddenly the spotlight swivels and shines on them, the congregation. What begins as christology abruptly becomes ecclesiology, and the Preacher's surprising point turns out to be a word about the church, how the faithfulness of Jesus brings worth and abiding value to the church and to its struggles to live the faithful Christian life.

Actually, the Preacher hints at this surprise from the start when he calls the hearers "brothers and sisters, holy partners in a heavenly calling" (3:1). At first, this sounds like a throwaway line, something conventional like "dearly beloved," but a closer look at this phrase reveals a doctrine of the church in miniature, one that will blossom into full flower as this section of the sermon proceeds. Indeed, three crucial aspects of the church's identity are compressed into this single address: the church is one, holy, and apostolic.

First, the church is *one*, a family of "brothers and sisters," a frequent way for early Christians to speak about each other (see, for example, Rom. 1:13; 11:25; 1 Cor. 12:1; Phil. 4:1; Col. 2:1; James 1:2; 1 Peter 5:9). Those in the Christian community are brothers and sisters not because of blood, or race, or even because they are fond of each other and share common opinions and interests. They are joined as one family because together they belong to Jesus Christ, who fully shared their humanity and "was not ashamed to call them brothers and sisters" (2:11, 17).

46

We often speak of the church as a "voluntary organization," some-thing that people choose or not, but the Preacher calls us to a more pro-found theological understanding of the church. In the deepest sense, we do not choose the church; we are chosen for the church by God. The church is not a club for people who are fond of religion; it is a commu-nity of people who have been summoned to a task, called to a ministry, given an identity in Christ, thrown together in mission. Clubs have membership rolls of companionable, like-minded people; churches, like families, include people who would never dream of being, working, and living together were they not "kin." Voluntary organizations have buffs and fans, and if the dues get too high or the demands too great, one can drop out, walk away, and find something more congenial. Churches, however, have "brothers and sisters" bound together in com-mon kinship to Jesus Christ, and the only way to walk away is to leave home.

Second, the church is *holy,* which is, of course, a tricky concept. The Preacher certainly knows that everyone who has spent more than a day around church people inevitably knows: the trees in the church's moral forest do not grow any higher than anywhere else. If greed in-fects the world, it poisons the church, too. If bigotry walks through so-ciety, it slithers its way along Church Street as well. The same goes for lust, pride, anger, sloth, and all the other deadly sins; the church is im-mune to none of them. Nevertheless, the Preacher dares to call the church holy because he knows that holiness is not an intrinsic human virtue but a divine gift. A scalpel is nothing but a knife until it is used by the surgeon for healing; a church is nothing but a collection of sin-ful people until it is gathered by the grace of God into seasons of wor-ship and acts of love.

The church is holy not because of the purity of its membership but rather because it is made holy by Jesus ("sanctified," 2:11). Jesus, through his own sufferings, knows every crevice of human weakness (4:15), and the living Christ is at work in the church, strengthening the community of faith beyond their own capacities for a ministry of mercy, service, and worship. In this sense, holiness is not so much a de-scription of the church's moral stature as it is a sign of how gracefully God puts the church to work in the world. The church is holy like the bread at the Lord's Table is holy; though quite ordinary, it is nonethe-less set apart for holy use and becomes the instrument of the extraor-dinary purposes of God.

Third, the church is *apostolic.* Customarily, this means that the church, in its ministry, teaching, and mission, stands in a great line of tradition faithfully passed on generation after generation from the

47

apostles to the present. Here the Preacher has something even more radical in view. The church is apostolic not only because it is connected to Peter, James, John, and Paul, but primarily because it is connected to Jesus, the first and true apostle ("apostle" as a title for Jesus is found only here in the New Testament). Thus Christians are "partners in a heavenly calling" that is not only grounded in a historical tradition but sustained in a living relationship to "Jesus, the apostle and high priest of our confession" (3:1).

The notion of ministry as "apostolic" signals that the church patterns itself after Jesus' own ministry. Just as Jesus was sent by God (the meaning of the term "apostle"), the church is sent to the world as well (see John 17:18). Just as Jesus is the "high priest" (a title the Preacher will later develop at length; see 4:14—10:18), the one who ascends to the holy place on behalf of humanity, so the church has a "priestly" ministry of loving service and compassion (see 13:3). Just as Jesus is the source and focus of "our confession," the church worships, teaches, and serves "holding fast to our confession" (see 4:14).

When the Preacher speaks of the church's "heavenly calling," this is not to gaze mistily toward some otherworldly "by and by" or to deny the church's ministry to human need in the here and now. To the contrary, it means that the church's faithful vocation in the present world is celebrated and validated "in heaven," that is, in the very life of God. This creates a radical freedom for the church since it is liberated from the need to justify itself on any "secular" grounds. What finally counts is not the balance sheet or numerical growth or how many programs take place in the family life center but faithfulness to the will of God.

Sometimes churches with strong budgets, professional music programs, well-equipped buildings, and the admiration of their civic communities can miss a deep truth: there is no real social justification for the church. It proclaims a word that is often not welcome, with a love that is easily scorned, to a world that is quick to be cynical, in the name of a Christ who was rejected and despised. Congregations with frail resources, meager programs, struggling ministries, sagging buildings, and not enough people to fill up the choir loft may more quickly understand that, finally, all the church has going for it is Jesus. The church is "apostolic" to the extent that it is responsive to the presence of Jesus in its midst. Wherever Jesus Christ, the pioneer apostle, is at work, however far-flung, the church is to follow, even if it limps as it goes; whatever Christ is doing, however demanding, the church is to roll up its sleeves and join in, even if its muscles are not so strong. Whatever truths Christ is teaching, however controversial, the church is to confess and proclaim them, even if it stammers as it speaks.

48

This implies that, though most ecclesiastical groups have elaborate networks of committees, boards, and assemblies, authentic decision-making about mission is not primarily a function of bureaucracy but of prayerful discernment and obedience. The church does not convene like a political party attempting to forge a platform or wrangle like a special interest group trying to muscle forth an agenda. Rather, the church seeks to listen to the Spirit, to discern where and how Christ is active in the world, and to become not managers of a religious organization but "holy partners in a heavenly calling."

More Glory than Moses (3:1b–3a)

The Preacher gets right down to the business of this section of the sermon by giving the congregation a listening assignment: "Consider that Jesus . . . was faithful to the one who appointed him" (that is, to God; 3:1–2). In other words, the Preacher grabs the congregation by the lapels and says, "Listen up and pay heed; the issue before us today is the faithfulness of Jesus."

But as soon he has their attention, the Preacher seems to change the subject, to shift from Jesus to Moses: "Moses," he states, "also 'was faithful in all God's house' " (3:2, loosely quoting Num. 12:7). It is as if he had said, "Babe Ruth was a *great* baseball player," and then immediately added, "but Ty Cobb was a great player, too." The rhetorical effect is that the congregation is holding the image of two faithful persons in their heads simultaneously, Jesus and Moses. This invites comparison, of course, and we can imagine the Preacher pausing just long enough for the congregation to figure the ratio before the Preacher confirms it: "Jesus is worthy of more glory than Moses . . ." (3:3).

Now, given the deep Jewish rootage of Christianity and the esteem granted to the figure of Moses, it seems a strange ploy for the Preacher to magnify Jesus by diminishing Moses. Why not work on the idea of Jesus' preeminence to Caesar or Plato or Herod instead? Actually, the intent is not to cast a shadow on Moses but to shine a light on Jesus. It was a stock topic in early Christian preaching to describe Jesus' superiority to key Old Testament figures, such as Abraham (see John 8:53), Jacob (see John 4:12), Solomon (see Matt. 12:42), David (see Matt. 22:45), and, of course, Moses (see 2 Cor. 3:7–18). The point was never to tarnish the luster of these giants but in fact to build on their greatness by conveying the truth that something greater even than Abraham or David or Moses is here.

So just as was the case in the earlier section of the sermon where the Preacher described Jesus' superiority to the angels (see comments

49

on 1:5–14), the Preacher is reworking an often-used and familiar sermon outline. The first readers of Hebrews would almost surely recognize the pattern, delight in its anticipated rhythms, and say "amen" to its christological claim. The purpose of this passage is not to attack Moses—indeed, Moses is presented in positive terms as "faithful in all" and will appear again later in the sermon as an exemplar of faith (see 11:23–28); the deeper goal is to present Jesus' strong and enduring faithfulness in sharp relief and to draw out the implications in the material that follows.

Turning the Jewel (3:3b–6)

A "jewel sermon" is the name homileticians give to a certain sermon strategy in which a preacher takes a complex idea and turns it slowly in the light, allowing the facets of the concept to glisten one after another. This is, in fact, the technique the Preacher now deploys. Notice that the allusion to Numbers 12:7 (3:2) contained a prominent image: the *house* of God. In Numbers, "God's house" is simply a symbol for the people of God, but the Preacher plucks this image out of its original context, transforms it into a jewel-like metaphor, and rotates it in the light.

First, he uses the image architecturally. Here, the "house" is a building, much as we may speak of a church building as the "house of God." Moses was certainly a part of this house, perhaps something like a main joist or a roof beam, but Jesus was the prime contractor in the construction. Moses was but a feature on the blueprint; God in Christ is architect and builder (3:3–4).

Then, while this tangible image of God's house hangs in the air, the Preacher turns the jewel to expose another facet. Now the "house" is not a building at all but something more dynamic: a living community, the household of faith. In the first century, a household could be quite large and diverse, with several generations of adults, many children, and a number of servants—in short, not a modern "nuclear family" but a complex and varied community. The Preacher invites us to imagine the whole history of God's people as one vast family, a spacious household embracing many generations—Abraham and Isaac, Deborah and Ruth, Jacob and Rachel—rolling forward to the present. Where do Moses and Jesus fit into this grand household of God? Moses was faithful *in* the house as a servant; Jesus, however, was faithful *over* the house as a Son, in charge of the house as the heir (3:5–6). Like a doorman whose job it is to announce who is about to enter the ballroom, Moses' job was "to testify to the things that would be spoken later" (3:5). This clear reference to Hebrews 1:1–2 puts Moses in the prophet's role, anticipating and pointing to the Son who was to come.

But there is one more turn of the jewel left, and herein lies the surprise. Now the "house" becomes the congregation itself (3:6). One might have expected the Preacher to add something here like, "Moses was a servant in God's house, and so are we." But no, the last turn of the jewel shines with an unexpected light; "we *are* his house." Dramatically, the Preacher has reminded the congregation that they are the very household of faith, built by God through and for Christ, a community of faith in which Moses (and all those things symbolized by Moses) function as servants. Moses was a part of this house and worked as a faithful servant in this house, but they *are* this house. When God in Christ built the house, what was being built was *them*, the household of faith, and Jesus the Son lives at home with them as their brother (2:11). Suddenly it dawns on the congregation that the Preacher is not only speaking of Moses in order to magnify Jesus, but he is also speaking of Jesus in order to magnify them, the congregation. They are the very house of God, governed, sheltered, and protected by Jesus the Son. As a pastor remarked when his church was destroyed by arsonists, "They didn't burn down the church. They burned down the building in which we hold church. The church is still inside all of us." The congregation now realizes that the way they were described in the opening phrase of this section, "brothers and sisters, holy partners in a heavenly calling" (3:1), was not a throwaway line at all but where this movement of the sermon was heading all along.

The logic of this overall passage can be seen when we recognize its chiastic shape:

A The identity of the congregation: brothers and sisters, holy partners (3:1a)
  B Jesus and Moses: both faithful (3:1b–2)
    C Jesus more worthy, because through him God built the house (3:3–4)
  B' Jesus and Moses: Moses is a servant in the house, Jesus a son over the house (3:5–6a)
A' The identity of the congregation: God's house (3:6b)

Chiastic structures function in several ways, but this text is an example of a transformative pattern, our understanding of A and B evolving into A' and B' by virtue of passing through the middle term C. In other words, something happens in C that transforms A and B into more profound versions of themselves, A' and B'. The pivot in this text

51

(C—Jesus is more worthy because God built the house through him, 3:3–4) not only elevates Jesus to the status of a son who is over the house, but it also elevates the hearers as well, disclosing that they, by virtue of being "holy partners," in fact are the very house built by God and governed by Christ the Son.

The final conditional clause ("if we hold firm the confidence and the pride that belong to hope," 3:6) is yet another example of a repeated ethical theme in Hebrews. The church is God's house by virtue of how it lives and serves. As the famed architect Frank Lloyd Wright once said, "When designing a house, you have to ask what the people want to live *in*, but you must also keep an eye on what they want to live *for*." If the congregation is to be faithful, if they are truly to be the house of God, enduring to the end, their faith must be anchored in that which is beyond the turmoil of the present circumstances. If they trust only what they can see, they are lost, set adrift. If, however, they hold firmly to and live for that which they have heard, that which can only be known in hope, then they can truly be the church with "confidence" and even "pride" (3:6).

Interestingly, the word translated "confidence" describes more than how someone feels; it describes how one *talks*, conveying the idea of free and bold speech that springs from assurance. The word translated "pride" (3:6) goes even farther, implying something like "boasting." So the Preacher began the sermon with God doing the talking (1:1–2), and now the church gets in on the act. When does the church engage in confident, even boastful speech? When it stands at the baptismal pool and proclaims over something as risky and unpredictable as a human being, "You have been sealed by the Holy Spirit in baptism and marked as Christ's own forever." When it sits down at the bedside of one in fevered pain and calmly reads the words of the psalmist, "The Lord is my light and my salvation, whom shall I fear?" When it stands at a graveside and is bold to say, "Do not let your hearts be troubled, and do not let them be afraid." When it audaciously says to those who would pollute the air and water, "The earth is not yours but the Lord's" and to those who would build walls between human beings, "Do you not know that God shows no partiality?" When it stands firm at crucial and perilous moments and, like Martin Luther King, Jr., bravely proclaims, "I'm not worried now. I've been up on the mountaintop. Mine eyes have seen the glory of the coming of the Lord." Because such speech surges forth from conviction about the trustworthiness of the promises of God, it expresses "confidence and pride" that belong not to arrogance, but to hope (3:6).

Learning to Rest Today

HEBREWS 3:7—4:13

We saw in the previous section that the congregation was surprised, and perhaps amazed and inspired, by the Preacher's disclosure that they are the very "house of God," built by God and ruled over by Christ. This is, of course, an exalted doctrine of the church, but the problem for the Preacher's congregation—indeed, for any congregation—is that it is very hard to believe this, really to believe it week in and week out, given the realities of church life. Here, knee-deep in the muck and mire of human struggle, this churchly "house of God," or at least the version of it that exists on the corner of Church Street and Main, does not appear very attractive or holy. Even in the most active parishes, people fall away; legs falter and hands droop; worship often seems stale and lifeless; conflicts emerge with maddening regularity; and the mission work is constantly in crisis. In truth, the church, the vaunted "house of God," looks to the naked eye more like a pup tent—frail, temporary, vulnerable, always at risk of having its stakes uprooted and being blown away.

Indeed, C. S. Lewis's quite articulate imaginary devil, Screwtape, advises his apprentice to tempt his human victim by playing on the inevitable disappointment that comes when the real and flawed church is compared to the pure and perfect church of the imagination:

> When [your victim] goes inside, he sees the local grocer with rather an oily expression on his face bustling up to offer him one shiny little book containing a liturgy which neither of them understands, and one shabby little book containing corrupt texts of a number of religious lyrics, mostly bad, and in very small print. When he gets to his pew and looks round him he sees just that selection of neighbours whom he has hitherto avoided. You want to lean pretty heavily on those neighbours. Make his mind flit to and fro between an expression like "the Body of Christ" and the actual faces in the next pew (C. S. Lewis, *The Screwtape Letters*, pp. 15–16).

In addition to experiencing the usual disenchantments over the church's shortcomings, the Preacher's congregation has an added reason

53

for discouragement: affliction. It is difficult to know precisely what happened, but some form of persecution, past or present, has caused the foundation of their faith to be shaken and the timbers of their confession to be weakened. They have "drooping hands and weak knees" (12:12), and the memory of abuse, hardship, and struggle is still fresh (10:32–34). Somewhere in the midst of this turmoil their possessions were plundered (10:34), but more important, their theological confidence was pillaged as well.

So the Preacher faces a disheartened congregation. They are tired: tired of the hassles of church routine, tired of the struggle, tired of serving, tired of being Christians. The grit of reality wears down faith. For these people, the so-called joyful Christian life has been little except turmoil and conflict; the alleged "house of God" looks and feels more like a house of pain.

To address their disillusionment, then, the Preacher must return to a crucial theme of this sermon: in the steadfast life of faith, appearances can be deceiving. Indeed, it has always been true that the promises of God do not look like they sound. The promise of a "holy nation" hangs by frail human threads, like imperiled Isaac, sly Jacob, and lustful David. The chosen and redeemed people of God look more like nomads than a nation, wandering in the wilderness, fearful of the journey, complaining of conditions, and yearning foolishly for the good old days in Egypt. The promised land, the land of milk and honey, feels more like a land of blood, sweat, and tears. The hoped-for Messiah, the Savior, turns out to be a rag-wrapped baby in a feed stall in Bethlehem, and the joyful life in Christ turns out to be full of resistance and saturated with suffering. The promises of God do not often look like they sound, and the question, thus, becomes once again: Should the church trust what it hears or what it sees—the gospel or the suffering?

Sabbath Rest (3:7–11)

To counter the congregation's disheartened weariness, the Preacher presents a brief, three-point sermon-within-a-sermon on the subject of "rest." This mini-sermon is based on Scripture, which the Preacher understands to be the living voice of the Holy Spirit speaking in the present (3:7). The Preacher's passage is Psalm 95:7b–11, which is quoted at length to the congregation (3:7–11), a choice of text that turns out to be fitting for two key reasons. First, the psalm connects to several themes the Preacher has already developed. For example, it employs as a negative example the disobe-

54

dience of the children of Israel in the wilderness, which provides an obvious connection to the emphasis on Moses in 3:1–6. Moreover, it lifts up the dangers of wandering and unfaithfulness, an earlier ethical theme (see 2:1–4) that the Preacher wishes to underscore. Also, the psalm includes the phrase "if you hear his voice" (3:7); the reference to hearing reinforces the Preacher's urgent claim that, in the battle between the eye and the ear, between what is felt to be true and the word reported by faithful witness, the ear must be privileged and the accent must fall on the hearing of the gospel and the believing of that which has been spoken (2:1).

Second, and perhaps most valuable to the Preacher, the psalm provides two rich theological terms—"today" (3:7) and "rest" (3:11)—which the Preacher uses as hooks upon which to fasten his message. In the Preacher's glossary, "today" refers not simply to the current date on the calendar, but more generally to the present tense in human experience. Every day is "today." In addition, "today" carries the sense of urgent time, the critical moment in terms of faith, the propitious time to decide: the *kairos,* the "eternal now."

The Preacher's use of "rest" is a bit more complex, integrating into a single term three significant themes. First, "rest" speaks of the beginning of time; it refers to the finished character of creation and draws upon the imagery of Genesis 2:1–3, where God is said to have "rested on the seventh day . . . from all the work that he had done in creation." Second, "rest" points to the end of time, to the finished work of redemption, when Christ is revealed as Lord; pain and toil are ended; death is defeated, and all that would destroy the will of God for human beings and for creation has itself been destroyed. Third, "rest" describes a possibility for the faithful in the middle of time, of those Sabbath Days in the life of God's people when the finished work of God is both remembered with thanksgiving and anticipated with hope. When the people of God enter the place of worship and sing confidently of the victory of God and when the people of God live ethically in the present crisis as those who are confident that God's triumph is sure, "today" becomes a "Sabbath rest."

These three dimensions of "rest" are gathered up in the familiar hymn "The Church's One Foundation" (Samuel J. Stone, 1866). The first stanza alludes to creation and describes explicitly the new creation in Christ.

> The Church's one foundation is Jesus Christ her Lord;
> She is his new creation by water and the word:
> From heaven he came and sought her to be his holy bride;
> With his own blood he bought her, and for her life he died.

In the middle stanzas, the hymn sings of the "rest" hoped for at the end of time:

'Mid toil and tribulation, and tumult of her war,
She waits the consummation of peace forevermore;
Till with the vision glorious, her longing eyes are blest,
And the great church victorious shall be the church at rest.

The final stanza describes the "rest" available as a Sabbath in the middle of time:

Yet she on earth hath union with God the Three in One,
And mystic sweet communion with those whose rest is won:
O happy ones and holy! Lord, give us grace that we,
Like them, the meek and lowly, on high may dwell with Thee.

In his farce, "God (A Play)," Woody Allen imagines a production of a classic Greek drama gone awry. The script calls for Zeus, Father of the Gods, to descend dramatically from "heaven," thunderbolts in full array, arriving just in the nick of time to save a confused and distraught humanity from self-destruction—*deus ex machina*. Unfortunately, as the actor playing the part of Zeus, trussed up in a harness, is being lowered to the stage, the wire attached to the apparatus gets wrapped around his neck, strangling the poor soul. Horrified by what has occurred, the cast falls into disarray. Finally one of the characters, attempting to pull things together, solemnly announces, "God is dead. . . . Ad-lib the ending" (Allen, pp. 141, 173–75).

In fact, according to the Preacher, attempting to "ad-lib the ending" to life's drama, to make up a story that seems in the moment of crisis to be better than God's script, is precisely the problem; it is what we do when we think that God is dead or absent or when we lose confidence in the trustworthiness of the promises of God. It is what we do in those inevitable seasons when the gospel seems too little to go on. As long as things go well, of course, remaining faithful is little challenge, but when trouble starts, when the storms of sorrow begin to rage, when the weeds of failure grow in the garden, when the valley of the shadow of death closes in, when the mouth goes dry in the spiritual desert, when all hell breaks loose, then we are tempted to ad-lib the ending, to trade God's story for one that is happier, easier, more upbeat, safer, less demanding, or at least one we can touch and see and hold in our own hands.

56 Exchanging God's story for another is an old and chronic problem. When Moses was interminably delayed on Mount Sinai, the people grew weary of waiting for a word that never came, for a leader who

never showed; so they coaxed Aaron to help them ad-lib a different ending. "Come," they said, "make gods for us . . . " (Ex. 32:1). When Jesus told the disciples that the road they were traveling led to Jerusalem, to great suffering, even to death, Peter immediately called for a rewrite of the script: "God forbid it, Lord! This must never happen to you" (Matt. 16:23). When Paul preached the gospel to the churches in Galatia, he was hardly out of town before the Galatians, having doubts and second thoughts, began tinkering with the story. "I am astonished," sputtered Paul, "that you are so quickly deserting the one who called you . . . and are turning to a different gospel" (Gal. 1:6).

The Preacher of Hebrews, too, knows about the human tendency to abandon the gospel for a more attractive story, knows that the real challenge for his congregation is to remain confident of and loyal to the promises of God in the muddled middle of things, when the time waiting for God's promised redemption seems overly long and there is precious little evidence around in the meantime to support faith. In a discussion of New Testament eschatology, theologian Christopher Morse noted, "What faith confesses to hear in the gospel . . . [is] a promise, as only God can make and keep, that even when the worst things come upon us that can possibly happen, they will not be able to prevent Christ's coming to us and to all the world in redemption, an ultimate reclaiming from all harm" (Morse, *Not Every Spirit,* p. 334). For the Preacher, the crucial task for the community of faith is to trust that promise, to be able with confidence to know that God is very much alive and at work, and, therefore, to stick to the plot, for the ending is sure.

Indeed, the Preacher thinks of God's story of creation and redemption as a long and sweeping drama involving numerous players. Human beings are morally free, and we can improvise lines and scenes, but the overarching plot is shaped by the design of God. What it means to be faithful is to harmonize all of one's actions to God's essential plot. On the seventh day, God, the playwright, rested, and the basic outlines of the plot were finished, complete, and perfect. We actors are told the plot and know where the play is surely going in God's providence, but we have been given the freedom to work our way toward this denouement.

The problem, however, is that the play is so long, the plot so complicated, so full of twists and unexpected turns, so ironic, so rich in tragic and painful moments, that it is easy to get lost, to get so caught up in one of the scenes that the outcome of the whole play is forgotten. Some actors become so weighed down in a tragic episode that they can't go on. Some, losing track of the plot, become disheartened and

57

abandon the play in the middle. Others, despairing of finding meaning in the play, begin to drift away from the plot. The cast is restless, sometimes in disarray, and the only way to keep us faithful, of course, is to keep reminding us of the basic plot. That is precisely what the Preacher in Hebrews is doing in his sermon-within-a-sermon.

Three Points
and a Poem (3:12—4:13)

The Preacher spins out three points in his sermon on the text from Psalm 95, and in the first of these (3:12–19) he points to Israel's failures in the past as a warning not to have "an evil, unbelieving heart that turns away from the living God" (3:12). In other words, do not, like our ancestors, doubt the trustworthiness of God and abandon the divine drama. Instead, members of the church, "partners of Christ" (3:14), actors in God's great drama should keep reminding each other of the whole script, should "exhort one another every day" (3:12, that is to say, every "today"). If they don't, the danger is that they "may be hardened by the deceitfulness of sin" (3:13).

Sin is depicted here as a liar, whispering in the ears of the church: "This play is going nowhere. God's drama is the theater of the absurd, without purpose or meaning. Don't kid yourself; all this pain and sacrifice and suffering is a waste. You can do better than this sad melodrama. Write your own play." No, warns the Preacher, don't write your own; don't be discouraged. Instead, remember how we rehearsed this play over and over in worship. You haven't gotten to the final scene; you cannot *see* it yet, but you have *heard* it spoken. Remember how it turns out at the last, and hold this first confidence to the very end (3:14). Don't be like children of Israel. They were being faithful to the script when they followed Moses out of Egypt, but out in the wilderness they lost confidence in the plot of the divine play and in God, and they rebelled. Thus they failed to make it to the final scene, to the place of rest (3:16–19; see Num. 14:20–23).

In the second point of the sermon (4:1–5), the Preacher reminds the congregation that, weary as they are, God's promise of rest "is still open" and cautions them not to fail to reach this goal (4:1). As we noted above, "rest" is a theological term expressing the will of God brought to completion. "Rest" points back to God's "Sabbath rest" when the good work of creation was finished, and it points forward to the completed work of redemption, when "every knee should bend, in heaven and on earth and under the earth, and every tongue should confess that Jesus Christ is Lord, to the glory of God the Father" (Phil. 2:10–11).

But "rest" is not just a concept applying to the beginning and the end; it is also a quality of Christian life in the middle of time, a calm assurance of participating in the will of God (4:3). Even now, as Christians struggle to be faithful in the midst of ambiguity and turmoil, the promise is that all of this counts, that their faithful actions are being gathered into God's everlasting purposes. In ways that are mysterious and beyond our full knowing, God uses the prayers and deeds of ordinary people of faith to redeem the whole creation. When all is said and done, the goodness of God will prevail and not evil; the love of God will triumph and not hate; the wholeness of God will overcome disease, and the Son of God will be on the throne and not the powers of death. And, here in the middle of history, to "rest" is not to stop working (that will come later; see 4:10) but to have the calm joy that one's labors are, by the grace of God, part of fulfilling this promise. God's "rest," then, is a gift of peace, a gift Jesus gave his disciples not on a cloudless day but in the dark night of betrayal; "Peace I leave with you; my peace I give to you. I do not give you as the world gives. Do not let your hearts be troubled, and do not let them be afraid" (John 14:27).

Such confident "rest" is a gift not easily received, however, and the Preacher sounds another note of warning, cautioning the congregation by again using Israel as a negative example. Both Israel and the church received the gospel (4:2), that is, both were given the script of God's story of creation and redemption. But the gospel "did not benefit [the children of Israel], because they were not united by faith with those who listened" (4:2). Who are "those who listened?" The language here is somewhat ambiguous, but the best understanding is that this statement refers to the church, and the Preacher seems to be saying that the gospel did not profit the children of Israel because they were not linked in faith to the church. Some have been tempted to understand this as a supercessionist claim, that is, as a product of the idea that the faithful church is God's replacement for a disobedient Israel. The notion is that God somehow erased the word "Israel" off the board and wrote "Christian church" in its place.

In truth, though, such a reading runs precisely counter to the Preacher's intent. Keep in mind that the Preacher is evoking the memory of Israel's failures to warn the church here, not patting the church on the back for being superior to Israel. Indeed, the Preacher's aim is to remind his congregation that the people of God, beginning with Adam and Abraham and flowing forward all the way to the end of time, form an unbroken chain of faith (see 11:1–40). No link in the chain stands alone; at no point along the way could any group of God's people say, "We are the complete and finished expression of God's will for human community"—not Israel and not the church, either. When our time comes in the divine drama, we are called upon to play out our part, to speak and act in the name of God, but the only sense that our momentary scene makes is as it is connected to the scenes that have gone before and to the ones that will come along after we have departed from the stage.

Israel's failure, then, is the same problem that threatens the Preacher's congregation: discouragement because they cannot see anything past their own role, their own moment in history. Israel rebelled, wandered from the script, lost confidence in God's redemption, and did not enter into God's promised rest because they failed to realize how their scenes in the play were connected to the full sweep of God's redemption, to the entire compass of the drama that eventually moves through Christ and the church to consummation.

But how could the children of Israel be expected to see this? In terms of human experience and vision, is there any way they could have anticipated the church? Yes, argues the Preacher, they could have by faith. It wasn't as if the script were unfinished or the outcome of the play in doubt. Indeed, God's "works were finished at the foundation of the world" (4:4). They couldn't *see* this, of course, but they could *hear* it in Moses and the prophets and the others who spoke the promise. By faith, they could have believed this promise of redemption, trusted that the play was moving steadily and surely toward a victorious finale. However, having gotten lost in their own difficult scenes, mistakenly thinking that the play was only about them and not about the whole of creation, having relinquished faith in the healing of all the nations and not believing what they heard about the victory of God over all God's foes, they wandered, rebelled, and lost hope.

There is no room, though, for the church to gloat over the failures of God's people in the past. The church is, of course, prone to the same temptation to faithless wandering, and this is the focus of the third point of the Preacher's sermon (4:6–11). The church needs to refresh its memory, to hear the full script again, and to believe it and act it out in their life together. When? Why, *today*, of course. The story is not over; the play is still running. It was not finished when Joshua took the people into the land (4:8); it was just getting going. This is "today," the urgent moment. As the words of the sermon fall on their ears, as the promises of the gospel sound out in the place of worship, the speech of God in the words of the Preacher create the crisis and demand of God's "today": "Today, if you will hear his voice, do not harden your hearts" (4:7). Those who hear God's voice once again get up on the stage of God's great redemptive drama, pick up their scripts, and be-

gin anew to speak their lines and play their parts. The roles are difficult; the demands are great. There is suffering to be endured, and
there are crosses to be borne. But there is also great joy because, when
we have heard the full script and been reminded of the Son victorious
over creation, we know that the drama is moving inexorably toward
that Sabbath rest where God will "guide them to the springs of the water of life, and God will wipe away every tear from their eyes" (Rev.
7:17). Those who hear and believe this promise experience even now,
in the middle of the drama, a foretaste of that rest. "Let us therefore
make every effort," intones the Preacher, winding up the third point,
"to enter that rest, so that no one may fall through such disobedience
as theirs" (4:11).

In time-honored homiletical fashion, the Preacher caps the three
points of his sermon-within-a-sermon with a poem, a hymnlike tribute
to the power of God's word (4:12–13). Sharper than any earthly two-
edged sword, the speech of God knifes through the curtain between
heaven and earth, piercing into the depths of humanity, exposing to
view the secret "intentions of the heart." This sword is so sharp that it
can separate even "the soul from the spirit," dividing between what really matters and what seems to matter. No one can hide from this
speech act of God; the word of God unveils every human life, laid bare
before the eyes of God. The word of God takes an ordinary day and
makes it "today," takes an ordinary moment and makes it the time of
crisis and decision, takes a routine event and makes it the theater of the
glory of God, takes an ordinary life and calls it to holiness. Human beings want to skip the casting call, leave the play early, wander in the
lobby at intermission, rewrite the ending. The living and active word
of God refreshes hope and restores confidence. The word of God turns
wandering human beings into principal actors in the magnificent story
of divine redemption, transforms frightened people who hide in the
garden and make excuses into holy partners of Jesus Christ who can,
through him, stand up boldly and render an account.

A Great High Priest

HEBREWS 4:14—5:10

As we have already seen, the Preacher employs in his sermon a fascinating array of homiletical strategies. In this passage, yet another of the preacher's techniques emerges into the light, in this case something like a sermonic "preview of coming attractions." The way this works is that the Preacher, in the middle of one section or "point" of the sermon, will give a quick glimpse of what is coming in a later "point," subtly placing in the minds of the congregation the anticipation of the first notes of what will eventually become a main theme.

The Preacher has used this preview technique before, albeit in a somewhat muted fashion. Here, though, we can see it on full display. Two chapters earlier the Preacher planted the seed, swiftly and briefly introducing the picture of Jesus as the "high priest" (2:17; 3:1). At that time, this christological title was left largely undeveloped, waiting to blossom in due season. Now the time has arrived, and beginning with Hebrews 4:14 and continuing all the way through chapter 10, the Preacher explores the high priestly identity of Jesus in rich detail.

What is the effect of this foreshadowing technique? Not only does it powerfully involve the readers by creating a sense of anticipation and fulfillment, it is also a means for the Preacher to communicate the rich complexity of his christology. In Hebrews, the christological identity of Jesus is a luxuriant tapestry woven from many theological cords. Jesus is given a number of christological descriptions—the divine Son, the suffering pioneer, the imprint of God's very being, the heavenly heir, the great high priest, among others. But this is not just a list of discrete titles; they are interlocking, overlapping categories. Yes, Jesus is the heavenly heir crowned with glory and honor, but he is at the same time the pioneer of faith who shares the full range of human suffering, and while he identifies fully with suffering humanity, he is even then still the divine Son, the reflection of God's own glory. In other words, all of the christological descriptions of Jesus are true and operative simultaneously, and the technique of planting one idea—like Jesus as the "great high priest"—while discussing another—like Jesus as the "faithful Son"—weaves a complex, multipatterned christological fabric.

62

Holding Fast and
Praying Boldly (4:14–16)

Standing in the background of the Preacher's sermon, it has already been noted, is a classic and often-preached Christian sermon
pattern: what we have called the "parabola of salvation" (see comments
on 1:5–14 and 2:1–4, and esp. figure 2, p. 27). In chapter 1 and again
in chapter 2, the Preacher traced the pathway of this parabola: Jesus
the Son traveled from the heavenly throne of God down into the
earthly realm, moved through history as a suffering pioneer, becoming
a full participant in human experience, and then swept triumphantly
back up into heaven where he is seated at the right hand of God.

Now in 4:14–16, he returns to this familiar arc again, but this is no
mere repetition, since each time the Preacher tracks the parabolic
course the accent falls on a different theological insight. The first time
through the parabola (1:1–4), the Preacher's goal was *confidence;* he
wanted to reassure the congregation that the shifting currents of human affairs, seemingly so random, chaotic, and hazardous, are in truth
presided over graciously by the divine Son, who is seated at the right
hand of God and who "sustains all things by his powerful word" (1:3).
The second time around (2:5–18), the Preacher's goal was *hope;* he
comforted the congregation by reminding them that Jesus, on the
downward sweep of the arc, joined himself fully and mercifully with
human suffering and, therefore, "he is able to help those who are being tested" (2:18). On this third pass through the parabola, however,
the Preacher's goal, intriguingly, is *prayer;* he seeks to encourage the
congregation toward a bolder and more vital prayer life by emphasizing that when Jesus the divine Son was traversing the parabolic arc he
was filling the role and performing the function of a "great high priest."

Indeed, the Preacher's main purpose in this section is to encourage the congregation toward daring, even audacious prayer, to "approach the throne of grace with boldness" (4:16). The Preacher wants
them to move past fearful prayers, tidy prayers, formal and distant
prayers toward a way of praying that storms the gates of heaven with
honest and heartfelt cries of human need. He does not want them to
pray like bureaucrats seeking a permit but like children who cry out in
the night with their fears, trusting that they will be heard and comforted. What the Preacher wants to say is gathered up in words of the
old hymn, "Have we trials and temptations? Is there trouble anywhere?
We should never be discouraged: Take it to the Lord in prayer! Can we

63

find a friend so faithful, who will all our sorrows share? Jesus knows our every weakness—Take it to the Lord in prayer!"

Even though the Preacher is focusing here on prayer, he knows that confident prayer is not merely a matter of technique. Ultimately, bold prayer is an expression of theological trust; the practice of prayer rests on what we believe about God and God's relationship to us. In short, how we speak our prayers of petition and intercession derives from how firmly we hold the creed. That is why the Preacher begins this section by urging that the congregation "hold fast to our confession" (4:14), that is, to the conviction that Jesus is God's Son, "the reflection of God's glory and the exact imprint of God's very being" (1:3).

How does the theological confession about Jesus empower bold prayer? First, it addresses the issue of the approachability of God. Sometimes contemporary Christians, schooled on a tame and domesticated picture of God, forget the sheer audaciousness of human beings daring to approach the holy, and thus we engage in prayer with all the casual nonchalance of ordering at a fast food restaurant. "God, I would like this and that," we say, as if we had every right to be speaking this way and as if God had every obligation to fill the order.

True prayer, however, is prefaced by awe. In prayer we dare to raise our voice to the Holy One, and thus all prayer is prefaced by the issue of divine glory and human unworthiness. Moses was compelled to take off his shoes in the presence of the holy (Ex. 3:5). Isaiah cried, "Woe is me," when he saw the Lord in the temple (Isa. 6:5), and the tax collector in Jesus' parable would not even look up to heaven, but beat his breast, saying, "God be merciful to me a sinner" (Luke 18:13).

Who is worthy to speak to God? Who is worthy to pray? The answer of the Christian faith, the answer of "our confession," is that no one is worthy, save Jesus, who was "without sin" (4:15), and the good news of the confession is that Jesus makes possible what we could not attain on our own. The claim that Jesus was "without sin" does not take away from his humanity; it in fact underscores it. Jesus embodied what God, in the creation, intended for human life. To say that Jesus is "without sin" is not to say that he was 99 percent human—human in every way except for the fact that he was without sin—but rather to affirm that Jesus experienced the full ambiguity and uncertainty, the weakness and the vulnerability, the temptations and the sufferings of life without compromising his humanity, without straying from his calling to be a human being. Thus he is our "great high priest" who opens up the way to God, and even more, he is our brother who gathers his sisters and brothers back into the very household of God.

The task of a priest is to approach God on behalf of the people, to gather what the people bring—their offerings, their prayers, the symbols of their repentance, their cares, their deepest needs—and to take these offerings into the very presence of God. The priest, therefore, faces in two directions. On behalf of the people, he faces toward God and travels to the holy place with their offerings. As the "great high priest," Jesus indeed turned his face toward heaven and traveled to God ("passed through the heavens," 4:14) on our behalf. Moreover, when Jesus turns toward God and places our offerings before God, he does not do so dispassionately. This high priest participates in human suffering; he "sympathizes with our weaknesses" (4:15). Therefore, Jesus does not place ordinary offerings—mere lambs or grains or money—on the heavenly altar; he carries, instead, the human condition to God. This high priest carries our need, our distress, our pain, our infirmities, our hunger for justice, our cries for peace to the very throne room of God.

But if the priest faces toward God on behalf of humanity, the priest also faces toward humanity on behalf of God. The priest represents God's holy presence among the people. What does the church see when it looks into the face of its great high priest? It sees in the face of Jesus "the reflection of God's glory" (1:3). It sees a God who stoops down from the holy heights to bear our griefs and carry our sorrows. It sees a God to whom it can pray freely, confident that we will "receive mercy and find grace to help in time of need" (4:16).

Jesus and the Job Description of High Priest (5:1–10)

So hanging in the air of the sanctuary is the Preacher's ringing claim that Jesus is the kind of great high priest who carries our deepest sorrows and most honest prayers to the very throne room of heaven, where we will find a banquet of mercy and grace.

But the Preacher knows that he is on marshy ground here, that this is the crucial theological and pastoral issue for his congregation. They know without a doubt that Jesus was weak—anyone with eyes to see could know that—but is Jesus also genuinely strong enough to help? They are well aware that Jesus was a fellow sufferer—every passerby who looked up at the cross could see that—but the question for them was whether this weak and suffering Jesus is also truly the divine Son who, in ways that eyes cannot see, stands in graceful glory at the beginning and end of time, and in the middle of time is even now redeeming the creation and bringing the children of God home.

65

In the Gospel of Mark, when the centurion saw Jesus die he exclaimed, "Truly this man was God's Son!" a statement that can serve as an expression of irony—"*That* is the Son of God?"—or as a statement of faith, or both. In similar fashion, when the Preacher announced that Jesus was the "great high priest," he knew the potential for irony; he knew that lying deep within his congregation is a weary resistance to this truth: "The suffering, rejected, defeated Jesus is a great high priest? Some great high priest."

How can the Preacher address this? All he has are words. Indeed, the gospel cannot be seen; it is hidden from ordinary sight and can only be heard. Faith comes by what is heard, and that is why the congregation must "hold fast to our confession" (4:14) and "pay greater attention to what we have heard" (2:1). The Preacher must use words to reinforce the truth that Jesus was, indeed, the great high priest.

He gives, then, a profoundly theological version of a standard speech delivered in many contexts, the "this is the right person for the job" speech. Whether spun out as a political candidate is being nominated to a convention or a new professor being proposed to a faculty or a CEO being suggested to a corporate board, the "this is the right person for the job" speech follows a standard pattern: it ticks off the provisions of the job description and shows how the person in question meets them, every one.

Here, in 5:1–10, the Preacher follows this pattern by describing, one by one, the qualifications for the Levitical high priesthood and showing how Jesus fulfills each of them. Indeed, the Preacher will describe how Jesus' credentials spill over the top, exceeding the demands of the Scriptures for the office of high priest. This point will not be lost on the congregation. Jesus is qualified in every way to be high priest, but he is not just a high priest; he is, in fact, the "*great* high priest." The former high priests were good people, but like any other human beings, life's hardships exposed their flaws. Jesus, on the other hand, was "made perfect" through the pain of life. Moreover, the former high priesthood was a part of a temporary order, something that God provided for a season in history. Jesus' priesthood, however, is for all time. It is this superiority of Christ to the former high priest that pushes the passage toward its dramatic climax: Jesus is "a high priest according to the order of Melchizedek" (5:10), a crucial but enigmatic claim that will be later elaborated in detail in 6:20—7:28.

66 The text is chiastic in structure, first listing three provisions of the job description of the ancient high priest, then, moving through the list in reverse order, describing how Jesus fulfilled, even exceeded, each of these (Attridge, p. 138):

A   The function of the high priest (v. 1)
   B   The person of the high priest (vv. 2–3)
      C   The appointment of the high priest (v. 4)
      C' The appointment of Jesus as great high priest (vv. 5–6)
   B' The person of Jesus as great high priest (vv. 7–8)
A' The function of Jesus as great high priest (vv. 9–10)

Taken as a whole, then, this text provides three sets of comparisons and contrasts:

1. *The function of the high priest* (5:1, 9–10). On the one side, there are those ordinary people who serve as high priest (those "chosen from among mortals," 5:1). Even though they are as human as the next person, their function nevertheless is to serve as mediators between God and human beings, straddling the gap between heaven and earth. In particular, the high priest takes the gifts and sacrifices of the people and offers them to God as an atonement for their sin (5:1). The high priest does not save the people from their sins—only God can do that; the high priest is but a messenger of salvation, carrying the symbols of repentance from humanity to God and returning with the good word of divine atonement.

Jesus, as high priest, also serves as mediator between God and sinful humanity, but Jesus exceeds the ancient priests in at least two key ways. First, he is not just the mediator, he is the *source* of salvation (5:9). Second, while the old priest had to keep going back time and again to the altar—new sins, new sacrifices—the salvation provided through the high priestly ministry of Jesus is *eternal* (5:9). Both of these contrasts anticipate themes that will be developed in detail in chapter 9. There Christ is presented as the source of salvation because, instead of bulls and goats he offered himself, a sacrifice without blemish. And Christ is described as offering eternal salvation because, unlike the annual and repeated atonement sacrifices of the priests, Christ offered himself "once and for all" (see 9:1–28).

2. *The person of the high priest* (5:2–3, 7–8). The ancient high priests were not merely liturgical functionaries who mechanically performed the duties of the priesthood; they were also pastors. To receive an offering from someone is to be given a symbol of the deep secrets of life: sin, guilt, fear, hope, hunger for salvation. The old high priests had a holy job, but they also needed to be compassionate people, sympathetic to human weakness. Because the old high priests were also ordinary human beings, their own weaknesses and failings enabled them to be sympathetic and to treat confused and sinful people with gentleness and understanding. Indeed, the sheer fact that the old priests

67

were every bit as sinful as their flocks meant that, as they approached the altar, they carried sacrifices for their own sins as well as for the sins of others (5:2–3).

Now, Jesus is the great high priest, but is Jesus also a good and compassionate pastor? Indeed he is. Jesus knows the pain and ambiguity of being human. Jesus embodies human life, including its frailty and limitation. The incarnation is the joining of the Son with the complete range of human experience, not avoiding agony and suffering. To impress this upon the congregation, the Preacher describes Jesus' suffering in powerful and graphic terms: "Jesus offered up prayers and supplications with loud cries and tears, to the one who was able to save him from death" (v. 7). By the Preacher's words, the congregation could see in their faithful imagination what they could not see with their naked eyes: Jesus as the great high priest, standing at the altar of heaven, offering to God the whole broken human condition, praying tearful, sorrow-drenched prayers to the God of salvation, prayers for himself and for all humanity.

This compelling image of Jesus praying tearful prayers immediately raises a question. When did Jesus do this? What moment in Jesus' life, "in the days of his flesh," is the Preacher describing here? Some have suggested that he refers to Jesus' anguished prayer at Gethsemane. Others, noting that the Gospels contain no single event that perfectly fits the Preacher's picture, argue that the Preacher is referring to the whole sequence of Jesus' passion and suffering. Most likely, however, the Preacher intends to recall the suffering prayers of Jesus from the cross, for example, "My God, my God, why have you forsaken me?" Psalm 22, from which the statement is drawn, speaks of cries to God in the midst of suffering (Ps. 22:2, 5, 24).

The Preacher's main point here is that Jesus through his suffering fulfills the pastoral role of the high priest. But here, too, the Preacher claims more—that Jesus surpasses the old priesthood. Jesus, like the old priests, was fully human, but unlike them his humanity did not erode into despair, loss of faith, and sin. Suffering is not sin; suffering is built into the human condition. Limitation and weakness are not sin; they, too, are part of what it means to be human. Jesus, as a human being, suffered and was limited and was weak, but his pain taught him obedience, not faithless despair (5:8); his frailty deepened his reverence for God rather than stiffening his rebellion (5:7). Pressed into the muck and mire of human anguish, Jesus never forgot that he was the Son. Therefore, not only is he compassionate toward those who have lost sight of the truth that they are God's very own children, Jesus can also take them by the hand and lead them home.

68

3. *The appointment of the high priest* (5:4–6). No ancient high priest was so presumptuous as to volunteer for the job or arrogant enough to try to grab some glory by appointing himself to the post. Instead, the high priest was called by God and served, like Aaron, by God's appointment (5:4).

Just so, Jesus too was not a self-appointed glory hound, but a high priest designated by God. The Preacher reinforces this point by quoting again two favorite psalms of Christian preachers: Psalm 2:7 and Psalm 110:4 (see comments on 1:3; 1:5; and 1:13, where these psalms are also cited). Once more, though, the fact that Jesus' high priesthood outshines the old priesthood radiates in the Preacher's words. Yes, Psalm 2:7 (5:5) conveys the message that Jesus was appointed by God, but it also conveys the extra measure of truth that this appointment was not merely to the priesthood but to *Sonship*. And yes, Psalm 110:4 also speaks the language of appointment, but here too there is a surplus. Jesus was appointed to be a priest not just for a lifetime, but "forever," and not according to the regular orders of the priesthood, but "according to the order of Melchizedek" (5:6). Once again, then, Jesus exceeds the job description of the high priest.

At this point, the congregation is probably not sure what the Melchizedek reference is all about, and the fact that it reoccurs in 5:10 simply heightens their curiosity. An explanation is required; the Preacher knows that. But he is content to leave them in suspense for the moment. The clarification will come in chapter 7, only after the Preacher has tantalized them for a while.

The Preacher as Crafty Teacher

HEBREWS 5:11—6:12

Suppose a teacher is about to introduce to her students a new and difficult idea, an idea that will require alertness and diligence to master. She is not sure, however, that the students are really up to the task. It's the middle of the term, and they are already growing weary. Also, they have struggled in the first part of the course with the more basic material. Will they have the energy, she wonders, for these advanced lessons? Plus, any new concept is always somewhat threatening, since it pushes aside familiar ways of thinking. Will the students simply dig in their heels and resist being disturbed by anything novel?

This teacher faces many obstacles, but she is determined to overcome them. She knows that what she wants to teach her students is demanding, but also very valuable, something they must learn if they are to continue growing. So, what should the teacher do? How can she coax these reluctant students to grapple with challenging new material?

One quite effective approach would be to use a bit of reverse psychology. She could start by telling the students that she has a rich and wonderful idea to teach them, but that, sadly, they just are not ready for it. She could close the textbook ruefully, shaking her head because they aren't wise enough, alert enough, or prepared enough to handle material this difficult, this important. Maybe some day, but not today; after all they are just babes in the woods, not really up to the stronger, adult stuff. Her goal, of course, would not be to shame them, but to motivate them. When they cried out in protest, their intellectual pride wounded, then she could, with a dash of feigned hesitation, agree to teach them this material since they insisted. If this tactic works, of course, the teacher will find herself presenting this new idea to a class full of eager, bristlingly alert students, bound and determined to prove to their teacher that she was wrong about them.

The Preacher of Hebrews employs a similar pedagogical and homiletical strategy in this section of the sermon. In the coming chapters of the sermon the Preacher plans to dive into deep christological water, and he wants to prepare his congregation for this plunge. The ideas ahead will be complex, challenging, even threatening, and he wants to focus their attention, to bring them to a new level of theological alertness and receptivity. So, like our example schoolteacher, the Preacher wakes up his sluggish students with a little reverse psychology, mockingly insulting the pride of the congregation so that they will take the dare and be willing to jump after him as he leaps into the theological depths.

The diving board from which the Preacher will spring was set up in the previous section of the sermon. There the Preacher developed the theme of Jesus' role as high priest, building gradually toward a christological denouement: "Although [Jesus] was a Son, he learned obedience through what he suffered and, having been made perfect, he became the source of eternal salvation for all who obey him, having been designated by God a high priest according to the order of Melchizedek" (5:8–9).

One could hardly find a single sentence that more comprehensively sums up the message of Hebrews. Indeed, this complex, many-layered claim stands at the theological heart of the sermon. If the

Preacher's congregation knows and believes and trusts the profound implications of this truth, they will be able to "lay aside every weight and sin that clings so closely and . . . run with perseverance the race that is set before us" (12:1). If, however, they remain spiritual children, wearing water wings and paddling around in the shallows, they will soon grow weary and drift away with the tide.

So everything is at stake. If the congregation is to move toward spiritual maturity, then they must become good and willing students; theological truths must be mastered and allowed to take root in their lives. The Preacher, realizing that the congregation faces a tough assignment, moves them from laggards at the back of the class to honor roll students on the front row in three steps:

1. *Too Dull to Get It* (5:11–14). The Preacher begins by playfully putting dunce caps on the congregation. He tells them that he has a lot more to tell them, but that it will be "hard to explain" and that they probably wouldn't be able to grasp it anyway. They are, he suggests, "dull in understanding" (5:11), and, what is more, they have already failed a few grades. They are still at the primary level, when they should have graduated and become teachers themselves (5:12). Moreover, they are like babies, morally immature, always demanding milk, when they should crave the solid food of ethical discernment (5:13–14).

It is important, of course, to recognize this as a rhetorical ploy. The author is speaking hyperbolically and somewhat facetiously (and will admit to this in 6:9). The goal in addressing the readers this way is not to push them down, but to lift them up and to stimulate their resolve to understand what follows. By calling them "dull in understanding," the Preacher desires, in fact, to sharpen their attention and to generate comprehension. The Preacher hopes that prodding his hearers as immature and fit only for pablum will have the effect of whetting their appetites for the substantive and lavish theological feast about to be served.

2. *No Turning Back* (6:1–8). Though one cannot see it on the printed page, there is a dramatic break between 5:14 and 6:1. Having playfully insulted the congregation by telling them they are too immature for the real meat of the faith, the Preacher pauses here long enough for the indignant protest to rise from the pews: "Hey, who do you think you're calling immature? How dare you suggest that we are too dull to understand this. Dish it out; bring on the theological meat!"

"All right," agrees the Preacher, confident that his strategy has worked, "let us go on toward perfection, leaving behind the basic teaching about Christ" (6:1). So here in step two the Preacher agrees to the tacit insistence of the congregation that he move beyond the basic course and proceed to the advanced christological lessons.

71

The announced aim to "go on toward perfection" is striking, since up to this point the language of perfection has been reserved for Jesus alone (2:10; 5:9). The notion that the readers are summoned to progress toward perfection is basically an invitation to imitate Christ, but not in the naive, mechanical sense. There is no thought in Hebrews of Jesus as merely a human being who lived a moral life and who serves as an attainable ethical example for Christians.

Throughout Hebrews, Jesus is the divine Son whose unique high priestly ministry accomplishes what no one else can do. Indeed, the unique character of the person and work of Christ makes possible all subsequent obedience on the part of the Christian community. Jesus is the pioneer to be followed, not simply a fellow traveler to be imitated. No one else could have blazed the trail. A Christian who faithfully imitates Jesus is like a pianist who plays Mozart well. If a critic observes that the pianist "played the piano concerto to perfection," it is, of course, an achievement of a different order than that of Mozart himself. The "perfection" of the performer depends upon that of the composer. So it is with the Christian life.

The Preacher indicates that the way to "go on toward perfection" is to leave behind "the basic teaching about Christ" (6:1). What does he mean by this? It is fairly clear that this "basic teaching" consists of the essential truths of the Christian faith, the material that would be imparted to someone who was becoming a new member of the Christian community. Indeed, the Preacher calls this material the "foundation" (6:1) and provides a summary of its content, no doubt reflecting the standard curriculum of instruction given to new converts in preparation for baptism: the need for repentance and faith, the meaning of baptism and the accompanying laying on of hands, and the promise of resurrection and final judgment (6:1–2).

Surely, then, the Preacher is not now urging the congregation to forget or repudiate these foundational truths. No, the Preacher is urging them to leave this basic teaching behind by going farther. Indeed, he is convinced that one cannot stay still in the Christian life. One must always be moving, and there are only two directions in which one can move: deeper or adrift. Either we keep growing, maturing, becoming more profound in our faith, or we are content to float lazily along the surface, unaware that the treacherous currents are pulling us more and more off course until we are hopelessly lost.

The possibility of drifting away prompts the Preacher to issue a solemn warning: "[I]t is impossible to restore again to repentance those who have once been enlightened . . . and then have fallen away" (6:4–6). These fearsome, seemingly irrevocable words appear to im-

72

ply that any believing Christian who subsequently lapses from the faith is forever a lost cause with no hope of restoration, no second chances.

There are clues, however, that the Preacher's warning, though surely stern, is not quite as severe as it may sound at first. To begin with, the Preacher's main goal seems to be to encourage his congregation, not to scare them. He realizes that his words are harsh, but he says, "Even though we speak in this way, beloved, we are confident of better things in your case" (6:9). In other words, the principal aim of painting a terrible picture of Christians falling away into disaster is to provide a motivational contrast between that dire predicament and the more hopeful circumstances of his congregation. He is saying, in effect, "But I am sure you will not veer from the truth. You will, I am confident, remain on course steady and true." The Preacher is like a parent trying to encourage a struggling teenager by saying, "You know, when a kid goes bad early, they stay bad. But *you* are a good kid, a really fine kid, and I am positive that you will work this out."

Second, it is very likely that the Preacher's lament over the impossibility of restoring lapsed Christians reflects a practical frustration in ministry rather than an absolute claim about the patience and mercy of God. When the Preacher says that restoration is "impossible," he is not pointing to limits on the grace of God; he is, rather, pointing to the actual and sad experience of his own church. Not only had the congregation experienced the loss and defection of previously steadfast adherents (see 10:32–39), they found that no amount of pleading and praying, working and worrying, could bring these people back into the community. Speaking realistically, for all practical purposes it was impossible to restore them to the fold.

People reject the Christian faith for all kinds of reasons. Some are alienated by the hypocrisy of the church and never make it past the front door. Some never have the chance to hear the gospel; others hear the gospel preached all the time, but not in a way that makes sense or speaks to their needs. Still others are persuaded that the faith is intellectually indefensible, a pious retreat from vigorous thought. There are many reasons why people turn away from the faith.

It is one thing when the Christian faith is rejected by those who do not know its depths and power, by those outside the church or those who have only skimmed the surface of the faith. Such refusal is sad, of course, but not necessarily tragic. When people push away what they do not fully know or understand, there is always the prospect that later they will see what they did not understand before, that discovery will lead to interest and interest to repentance and renewal.

73

It is far more tragic, however, when the faith is rejected by those who do know its depths, those who "have tasted the heavenly gift." To paraphrase the Preacher (6:4–6), when those who have profound insight about the gospel, who have experienced grace in the depths of their lives, who have discerned that they are guided and comforted by God's Spirit, who have heard God speaking to their hearts, and who have been given a peace that the world cannot provide—when such as these turn their backs on the faith, it is a grievous and seemingly irreparable tragedy. They are not walking out on what they do not understand, but from what they do understand. They fall away not because they have never tasted the mercy and love of God, but in spite of the fact that (maybe even because) they have. When they slam the church door, they are not turning their backs on the church; they are storming away from grace; in effect, says the Preacher, they are "crucifying again the Son of God" (6:5).

Every pastor knows about this, and the Preacher is a pastor. The Preacher knows the travail of the life of faith. Even though we wish that every story had a happy ending, not all of them do. Some people in a congregation are like fertile ground; the rain of God's blessing falls on them, and they blossom forth with a bumper crop of gratitude and service. Other people, however, are like poor soil; no matter how thoroughly the rains of mercy soak the land, all that comes up are thorns and thistles (6:8).

3. *Prize Students* (6:9–12). Now, having rebuked the pupils into attention and warned them of the perils of drifting away, the Preacher is ready and able to praise them. Having impressed upon them the dangers and the demands of Christian maturity, the author wants to supply encouragement. When all is said and done, they have what it takes to endure. Others may fall away, but the Preacher is confident that the readers will not be among them. After all, they have worked diligently and served lovingly in the past and the present alike (6:11).

So the Preacher who began this passage by poking fun at his dull congregation ends with a flourish, encouraging the congregation toward maturity, to bear down and to attend to the word being proclaimed to them. Indeed, the Preacher underscores how they have quickly moved to the head of the theological class. Those who at the beginning of this section were described, in a mock scold, as poor students, stuck in the first grade, are here, astoundingly, prepared for graduate school. They are ready to "realize the full assurance of hope to the very end" (6:11). Initially the readers were called "dull in understanding" (5:11). Now, the Preacher, playing on the very same Greek word, expresses confidence that the hearers will not be dull

74

(NRSV = sluggish), but will in fact be "imitators of those who through faith and patience inherit the promises" (6:12).

This last phrase raises two main questions. First, when the Preacher names "those who through faith and patience inherit the promises," whom does the Preacher have in mind? Who are these people that the readers of Hebrews are to imitate? Some have suggested that the Preacher is referring specifically to the Old Testament patriarchs, Abraham in particular. This position is reinforced by the fact that the author moves in the next section (6:13–20) to an explicit discussion of Abraham. Others have seen 6:12 more broadly as a reference to the whole history of God's faithful people. It stands, then, as an anticipation of the roll call of the faithful in 11:1–39. Still others have seen this phrase as having a more contemporary referent, namely that the readers are to imitate the stronger ones in their own community, the ones who have not slackened in their faith and endurance. Some confirmation of this can be seen in 13:7, where the readers are urged to "remember your leaders" and to "imitate their faith."

There is probably no reason to choose any one of these options over the others, since the Preacher almost surely means to suggest all of them. The author thinks of God's people as those whose lives are gathered up into the great narrative of God's salvation, as those who, throughout history, have heard the promise of God, believed that promise, and lived their lives trusting it. This faithful stream began with Abraham, broadened into a river of God's people in Israel, surged forward most mightily in Jesus, and now courses through the church. The readers are to fasten their attention upon those who had a vision of God's ultimate triumph, and who, because of this vision, kept putting one foot in front of the other as they slugged it through, knee-deep in the muck and mire of the pilgrim way. Because they trusted the promise and hoped in the triumph, they were able to be patient in adversity. The Preacher wants the hearers to imitate these faithful people and, thus, to join them as inheritors of the promise.

That leads to the second question: What, for the Preacher, are "the promises?" Again, the Preacher surely understands this category in both narrow and broad ways, both as specific content and as a more encompassing theological dynamic. In the narrower sense, at various points along the way in the story of salvation God made very specific promises: for example, the promise to make Abraham a great and blessed nation (Gen. 12:1–3), the promise to bring the children of Israel into a land flowing with milk and honey (Exod. 3:8), and the promise to make a new covenant with the house of Israel

75

(Jer. 31:31–34). In the broader sense, however, it is the general character of God to make and keep promises; God is a promise-making and promise-keeping God. In all times and places, the promise is: "Follow the path of obedience and faith, and I will bring you to a place of rest and joy." Many have followed that path, none more excellently than Jesus. Now the readers of Hebrews, prize students, those who belong to Christ, are being urged to put one foot in front of the other along the pilgrim way. The Preacher exhorts them to trust the promise of rest and triumph and to be patient.

The Sure and Steady Promises of God

HEBREWS 6:13–20

Now that the Preacher has used a bit of reverse psychology to rouse the congregation's resolve (5:11—6:12), he is ready to shower them with some positive theological affirmation. The Preacher, about to embark on another phase of this difficult christological adventure, made the hearers want to pay attention to this teaching by wounding their pride, by suggesting—somewhat tongue-in-cheek—that they may be too dull to understand the complexities of Jesus' high priesthood (5:11). Now the Preacher announces the plus side of putting on their theological thinking caps. Those who discern and hold onto the profound gospel truth of Jesus' high-priestly role will be given the key to hope. They will be able to endure, living patiently the life of faith all the way to the end, and will become inheritors of the promises.

The very mention of the promises (6:12) forms a homiletical connection to the story of Abraham, to the story of the beginning of God's ongoing activity as the maker and keeper of promises. In order to encourage them in their advanced lessons, the Preacher now beckons the congregation to draw closer as he tells them the story of the good things that happened to Abraham.

God Swears (6:13–18)

76

This passage is based upon the custom in oral cultures of swearing, or oathtaking. In the ancient world, whenever people wanted to guarantee their promises or give solemn value to the trustworthiness of their words, they would swear by the divine name. Philo states that "an oath is an appeal to God as a witness on some disputed matter" (*De Sacrificiis Abelis et Caini* 91–94). If two people were in disagreement on a matter of trust—word against word—one of the parties could up the stakes by uttering an oath, thus summoning the divine presence and saying, in effect, "If I am not telling the truth, may the gods do to me as I deserve." In a world where speech and act were intimately connected, to swear a divine oath was to play the ultimate chip, to put oneself at risk by raising a verbal lightning rod and declaring, "You can believe my word, and I swear, if I'm telling a lie, strike me down."

Although in the contemporary world of tamer speech and written contracts oral oathtaking has largely disappeared, one can still find it here and there, for example when a child puts her hand over her heart, saying "I cross my heart and hope to die," when a barroom debater raises his hand and vows, "As God is my witness," or when a couple at their wedding makes their "solemn vows." In a more formal legal sense, a witness in court takes an oath: "Do you solemnly swear to tell the truth, the whole truth, and nothing but the truth, so help you God?"

The Old Testament did not prohibit such oaths, but required that they be taken only in Yahweh's name (rather than swearing by some alien god; see Deut. 6:13). To break an oath made in God's name was, of course, a serious offense, not only against the truth but also against the character of God; therefore, a curse is pronounced upon swearing falsely (see Zech. 5:3–4).

It is against this background of oaths and swearing that Hebrews discusses the steadfastness of God's promises. Human beings, the author reminds us, always swear by some greater power (v. 16). They place their hand on the Bible, direct their gaze to heaven, invoke the name of God, or say "cross my heart and hope to die." God, of course, is not able to swear by any greater power. So when God wanted to let Abraham, and all who would follow him, know the trustworthiness of the divine promise, God "swore by himself" (v. 13).

This idea of God swearing by God's own name probably reflects a popular Jewish exegesis of Genesis 22:16, one that was popular in hellenistic synagogue sermons (Attridge, *Hebrews*, p. 179; Lane, *Hebrews 1—8*, p. 149). God made the promise and also swore by his own name; in other words, God made a firm promise and issued a warranty as well. These "two unchangeable things" (6:18)—the promise itself and the accompanying oath—are unshakeable assurances to the congregation of the impossibility that God would go back on the promise. How

77

should the congregation respond? Exactly as Abraham did: he "patiently endured" and, therefore, "obtained the promise" (6:15).

Hope:
The Anchor of the Soul (6:19–20)

Here the Preacher reveals why so much energy has been expended establishing the trustworthiness of God and the sure and unchangeable character of God's promises: Christian hope is anchored in those promises and depends upon the unshakeable reliability of God.

There is a revealing scene in Tom Stoppard's play *The Real Thing*, where a husband and wife are having one of those marital conversations that are superficially playful but underneath full of treachery and danger. The husband is badgering his wife to reveal whether or not she has really been faithful to him during their marriage. He wonders aloud if she has ever taken a lover. Finally, she blurts out the truth, yes:

> The husband tries to be brave. "Well . . . how many—um—roughly how many—?"
> "Nine," she replies.
> "Gosh," he exclaims, after a startled pause.
> "Feel betrayed?" she asks.
> "Surprised. I thought we'd made a commitment."
> "There are no commitments," she retorts, "only bargains."
> (Stoppard, p. 64)

In a world where there are truly no commitments, only bargains, there can be no lasting hope, only a ceaseless jockeying for personal advantage. The Preacher, however, knows that God has made an enduring commitment, not a flimsy bargain but a trustworthy promise, to sustain and redeem creation. Those who rest in that firm promise can truly possess hope.

In 6:19–20, the Preacher sings a doxology about hope. We should trace the lines and phrasing of this passage slowly and carefully, since the Preacher takes the liberty of mixing metaphors. In simple terms, hope is pictured as a cord attached to an anchor. The anchor has been taken by Jesus, "a forerunner on our behalf" (v. 20), up into heaven itself, the secret place of God ("the inner shrine behind the curtain"; v. 19), and has been fastened securely to the throne of God. The anchor, therefore, holds secure because it is attached to the steadfast commitment of God, the God who keeps promises.

The cord extends from heaven's heights back down to earth, where faithful people can "seize the hope set before us." Like rock climbers scaling an imposing height, Christians steady themselves by trusting God's promises, holding on for dear life to this cord of hope.

78

This image of the cord and the anchor was no doubt drawn from the homiletical stock of the synagogue, and it can still be found in contemporary Judaism. Martin Buber, for example, spoke of Jewish hope when he declared, "There are no knots in the mighty cord of our Messianic belief, which fastened to a rock on Sinai, stretches to a still invisible peg anchored in the foundation of the world" (Martin Buber, quoted in Simon, p. 26). For Buber, the cord of hope is stretched between Mount Sinai and the world's foundations.

For the Preacher of Hebrews, the cord of hope spans the distance between the creation of all things through Christ and redemption of all things in Christ. It is attached to heaven on each end, swooping down through human history. In other words, the now familiar arc that traces the parabola of salvation is depicted in physical terms, as if it were a cable of hope passing through history, to which the congregation is urged to hold on for dear life:

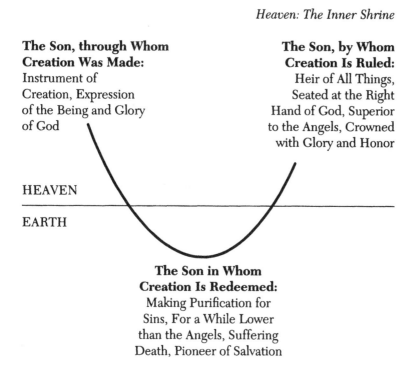

Heaven: The Inner Shrine

The Son, through Whom Creation Was Made: Instrument of Creation, Expression of the Being and Glory of God

The Son, by Whom Creation Is Ruled: Heir of All Things, Seated at the Right Hand of God, Superior to the Angels, Crowned with Glory and Honor

HEAVEN

EARTH

The Son in Whom Creation Is Redeemed: Making Purification for Sins, For a While Lower than the Angels, Suffering Death, Pioneer of Salvation

79

Figure 4

In describing Christian hope as anchored in heaven, the Preacher speaks of heaven as "the inner shrine behind the curtain," imagery drawn from the wilderness tabernacle (see Ex. 26:31–35). In the actual tabernacle, only the high priest could go into the sacred space of the inner shrine. The Preacher connects this to Jesus, who has entered the heavenly sacred space on our behalf. This connection allows the Preacher to identify Jesus as "a high priest forever according to the order of Melchizedek," thus both completing the inclusio that began at 5:6 and introducing the theme of the next four chapters of the sermon.

The High Priesthood of Jesus: Advanced Course

HEBREWS 7:1—10:29

At long last, the preacher turns to the discussion promised back in 5:11: the more detailed and difficult exploration of the concept of the high priesthood of Jesus. The basics of this topic had been introduced in 4:14—5:10, but now the Preacher moves from arithmetic to calculus, from the elementary to the advanced, or, as he would put it, from "milk" to "solid food" (5:12–14).

As we have seen, the Preacher, aware that he has "much to say that is hard to explain" (5:11) and concerned that the congregation could well get bogged down here, paused, in the previous section, to engage in a long and occasionally playful digression in which he told them not to get sleepy and check their watches but to pay careful attention for the sake of theological growth and maturity (see comments on 5:11—6:12). Now the time for the long-anticipated christological advanced course has come. After an extended windup, the preacher is finally ready to make the pitch.

We can certainly understand why the author hesitated. Reading through chapters 7—10, one can see why the preacher was concerned about the congregation's readiness to absorb this material, since the reader is now treated to a lengthy and sustained piece of christological analysis spanning four theologically demanding, biblically rich, structurally complex chapters. To the modern eye, this section of Hebrews seems particularly hard to follow, even more ornate and labyrinthine than usual.

We must keep reminding ourselves, however, that Hebrews was not written for the eye, but for the ear. Or perhaps more accurately, it is an example of prose built according to acoustical logic; it is shaped the way the ear likes to hear rather than the way the eye likes to read. This is not a theological textbook in which issues are presented in a straightforward manner; it is a sermon. It doesn't move in a straight line; it weaves, spirals, and doubles back. Making one's way through this section of Hebrews is less like tracing the lines of a legal argument and more like listening to a symphony. In the middle of one movement, devoted to a major theme, a minor theme will be introduced—something like a single line played by an oboe, winding its way like ivy through the lattice of the dominant motif. In the next movement, however, the themes are reversed. The oboe line now assumes control, taken up with force by all of the strings and the brass, and what was previously the major theme is muted, sounded only as a faint memory by a lonely bassoon.

This is not to say that there is no underlying pattern to this section of Hebrews. First, despite the twists and turns, there is thematic unity here; the Preacher never wavers from his assigned topic of Jesus as "the great high priest." Indeed, chapters 7—10 seem to constitute yet another "sermon-within-a-sermon" (like 3:7—4:13), this time one in which the Preacher chases the idea of Jesus' priestly ministry through three key Old Testament texts: Psalm 110:4; Jeremiah 31:31–34; and Psalm 40:6–8. Sometimes, though, the unity of this miniature sermon is difficult to spot since the Preacher leaps acrobatically from idea to idea rather than employing a simple, expository, one-two-three logic. The three Old Testament texts are related and intertwined through a familiar rabbinical preaching method in which the preacher, like a child on a playground gym set swinging from one bar to the next, swivels from text to text on the basis of overlapping words and themes, often to the wonder and delight of the hearers.

Second, when we x-ray this sermon, we are surprised to discover that all of these pulpit gymnastics and homiletical calisthenics are performed on a very sturdy frame. At the foundational level, the design of this sermon-within-a-sermon, though quite elaborate, is nonetheless clear and predictable. It is divided into five sections: each of the first four is composed of a list of claims about the *old* priestly order followed by a matching set of claims about the *new* and superior priesthood of Jesus. The division between the old and the new runs like a spine down the middle of this lengthy passage, and the Preacher shuttles back and forth, saying, in effect, "Look at the old priesthood, the old law, the old covenant, the old sacrificial system; compare it with the new priesthood, the new law, the new covenant, the everlasting sacrifice of Jesus." The fifth and last section resides entirely on the "new" side, as if to indicate that, after weaving back and forth between old and new, we finally end up living and worshiping under the new covenant:

81

INTERPRETATION

OLD	NEW

I. The Priestly Order of Melchizedek 7:1—8:13

A. 7:1–3 The identity of Melchizedek, who "resembled the Son of God"

A'. 7:13–17 The identity of Jesus, who "resembled Melchizedek"

B. 7:4–10 The greatness of Melchizedek, who was superior to Abraham, and even in the old order, a departure from the Levitical priesthood

B'. 7:18—8:6 The greatness of Jesus as high priest, "perfect forever," author of "a better hope" and "mediator of a better covenant"

C. 7:11 The imperfection of the old priesthood and the need to look for the new

C'. 8:7–12 Fault with the first covenant and the need to look for the second

D. 7:12 A new law

D'. 8:13 A new covenant

II. Priestly Worship, Old and New 9:1–15

E. 9:1–5 The old sanctuary

E'. 9:11 The "greater and perfect" new sanctuary

F. 9:6–10 The actions of the old high priest, which cannot perfect the conscience

F'. 9:12–15 The actions of the new high priest, which bring eternal redemption

III. Death and Purification 9:16–28

G. 9:16–22 Purification through death in the old covenant

G'. 9:23–28 Purification through the death of Christ

IV. The Benefits of the Priestly Ministry 10:1–18

H. 10:1–4 The old, repeated sacrifices

H'. 10:5–18 The "once for all" sacrifice of Christ

V. The Worship of the New Covenant 10:19–39

I'. 10:19–25 Getting ready to go to worship

J'. 10:26–39 Warnings and encouragement

The purpose of this long section is, of course, to sing a hymn of praise to Jesus Christ, the "high priest of the good things that have come" (9:11), but the Preacher has a practical goal in mind as well. He is not conducting a doctoral seminar on christology; he is trying instead to renew the congregation's hope and endurance. Through baptism, they belong to Jesus Christ; the forgiveness, peace, and harmony with God achieved through the priestly ministry of Jesus are great gifts given to them. Because of this, they can worship with joy and confidence, confess their faith with boldness, find meaning in the fellowship of the church, perform acts of mercy and kindness, and, most of all, keep on hoping and serving with joyful confidence in the faith. In short, what seems at first glance like a long and complex journey through the winding corridors of high priestly christology turns out in the end to provide cooling refreshment to weary Christians in the everyday living of the Christian life.

The Priestly Order
of Melchizedek (7:1—8:13)

A. *Melchizedek, Who Resembles the Son of God* (7:1–3). As we noted earlier (see comments on 4:14—5:10), the Preacher's discussion of Jesus as the "great high priest" employs the strategy of foreshadowing. The Preacher played the first few notes of the melody way back in 2:17 and 3:1, but only later—at this point in the sermon—do we hear the full tune. This is, however, no mere homiletical technique; rather, it is a reflection of the theological reality being proclaimed. The Preacher foreshadows the great high priest in the sermon in the same way that God foreshadowed the great high priest in history. Long before Jesus served as the great high priest, the Preacher claims, there was a harbinger of things to come in the form of the enigmatic figure, Melchizedek of Salem, who gave a blessing to Abraham and received a tithe in return (7:1–2).

Who was Melchizedek? In terms of strict biblical criticism, that is a good question. He appears only twice in the Old Testament, a vague reference in Psalm 110:4 and a curious story about the above-mentioned meeting with Abraham (then Abram) in Genesis 14:17–20. In the Genesis passage, Abram, returning from a military victory, encounters the King of Sodom, but before any interaction can occur between them, a somewhat strange interruption in the action occurs. King Melchizedek of Salem, who is described as "priest of God Most High" (probably a reference to a Canaanite god), abruptly shows up on the scene, brings

83

out bread and wine, and gives Abram a blessing in the name of this "God Most High." Abram responds by offering Melchizedek "one tenth of everything," and then Melchizedek disappears from the story as suddenly and mysteriously as he arrived. Psalm 110:4 only fuels the mystery since the phrase "you are a priest forever according to the order of Melchizedek" simply appears there, without elaboration or explanation.

The Preacher is not a historical critic, however, and he is not at all occupied with the modern concern to know what facts lie behind these Old Testament references. Indeed, the Preacher's Melchizedek is not the obscure holy man for some minor Canaanite deity who wandered out of the desert to make a cameo appearance in Genesis, but the "homiletical Melchizedek," that is, the Melchizedek who was the product of Jewish and Christian preaching and who appears fairly frequently in Jewish and Christian literature around the first century. This "homiletical Melchizedek" was something like the "three kings" of countless Christmas pageants, an amalgam of biblical material and popular piety. The Old Testament references to Melchizedek are elusive, spare on detail, so preachers were happy to fill in the gaps. The Preacher of Hebrews borrowed some of these sermon notes on Melchizedek from others, and he may even have supplied some new musings of his own. It is difficult to determine how much of what the Preacher says about Melchizedek is a part of the standard lore, already familiar to the congregation, and how much is newly wrought, a product of the Preacher's creative exegetical imagination.

In any case, the Preacher's point about Melchizedek is quite clear. He proclaims that way back on the old side of the ledger, back in the days of Abraham, back before the Levitical priesthood ever was, there appeared a foreshadowing of Jesus, the coming great high priest. This foreshadowing was, of course, Melchizedek, and who was Melchizedek? In the Preacher's perspective, he was a priest of the true and living "Most High God" (7:1) whose name—Melchizedek, King of Salem—means "king of righteousness" and "king of peace." This anticipates, of course, Jesus' messianic role as the king of righteousness and peace (7:2). Again, though, the Preacher is following homiletical fashion more than strict etymology, since "Melchizedek" in all probability literally means "my king is (the Canaanite god) Zedek" (Attridge, p. 189).

According to the Preacher, Melchizedek anticipated Jesus not only by having an interesting, theologically significant name, he is also a forecast of things to come by virtue of his rare and noteworthy lin-

84

eage—or, rather, his lack of one. Melchizedek, claims the Preacher, had no father or mother and, therefore, no genealogy. What is more, as a consequence of having no parents and no pedigree, he was eternal, without either a beginning or an ending in time (7:3).

Where did the Preacher get that idea? The ancient rabbis had a principle of biblical interpretation that asserted that all truth was in the Scripture. So, as they said, "What is not in the Torah is not in the world." Now, the Scripture does not anywhere mention Melchizedek's parents, and, according to this rabbinical principle of interpretation, this is not merely an omission but an indication that Melchizedek never had any parents; they were not in the Torah so they must not have been in the world. Once that piece of logic falls, only a few more dominoes have to topple before we can say that Melchizedek was a timeless, eternal character.

While such reasoning may strain contemporary readers of Hebrews, it all made perfectly good sense to the Preacher's congregation, and besides, the main point of all this is not really about Melchizedek *per se* but rather how the qualities seen in him—righteousness, peace, and timelessness—point forward to the nature of Jesus, the true and perpetual great high priest. Theologically, the Preacher wants to say that Melchizedek is a signpost planted in the old order indicating that the good gifts given to humanity in Jesus were there in God's mind from the very beginning. "In these last days," said the Preacher in the sermon's opening sentence, "God has spoken to us by a Son," and now he adds that this graceful and saving Word from God "in these last days" was not an afterthought. It was always there in the providence of God, and, if we knew how to listen for this divine Word, we could have heard the first syllable uttered long ago in Melchizedek.

Like the wedding miracle at Cana, Jesus is God's very best wine, saved for the last but ready from the dawn of creation. There were foretastes of this magnificent vintage, indeed—most remarkably in this impressive and elusive figure Melchizedek, who was an anticipatory sip poured into the glass of the old order. Melchizedek was the bouquet of the wine yet to come. He was a king of righteousness, a king of peace, a priest forever who had no beginning and no end. In other words, Melchizedek "sounds like" the great Word to follow; he is a foreshadowing of the great high priest to come, a human being who "resembling the Son of God . . . remains a priest forever" (7:3).

B. *See How Great Melchizedek Is!* (7:4–10). Having introduced the congregation to Melchizedek, the Preacher now engages in a bit of inventive exegesis on Genesis 14:17–20 in order to show how Melchizedek, the priest from nowhere with no genealogy, was greater

85

even than Abraham, the father of all, and all the official priests of the Levitical line.

He rifles through the Genesis story and finds two pieces of evidence for the superiority of Melchizedek: the blessing and the tithes. In regard to the first, Melchizedek blessed Abraham, and, as the Preacher says, "It is beyond dispute that the inferior is blessed by the superior" (7:7). Actually, there may be some room for dispute here since there are some biblical examples of the opposite—inferiors blessing superiors—as when King David was blessed by his servant Joab (2 Sam. 14:22). But we get the Preacher's point nonetheless: Melchizedek, as the one doing the blessing, was thus in a position of superiority even to the great Abraham, the one "who had received the promises" (7:6).

In regard to the tithes, the Preacher points out that the Levitical priests are commanded by the law to collect tithes from their kindred (7:5; see Num. 18:21–32). Melchizedek, however, who had no law to back him up and who was not even kin, collected tithes from no less a notable than Abraham. Where did he get the power and authority do do that? It was because he is "a priest forever" (7:3). In contrast to the Levitical priests, who were mortal, Melchizedek is immortal, "one of whom it is testified that he lives" (7:8).

Like most pulpiteers, the Preacher cannot resist a small joke along the way. He quips that "one might even say" that, when Abraham paid the tithes to Melchizedek, Levi himself, the very head of the priestly tribe, paid these tithes as well, since at the time he was still in Abraham's loins (7:9–10). The punch line implies, of course, that when Abraham was placing those tithes at Melchizedek's feet, Levi was also filling out a tither's pledge card, since he was latently present in Abraham's seed. The way the Preacher introduces this witticism (with a "one might even say" and probably a wave of the hand) indicates that it is an aside and not to be taken with great gravity. Indeed, someone could well point out that, technically speaking, Jesus was in Abraham's loins, too—a somewhat awkward obstacle to the Preacher's argument!

C. *The Imperfect Old Priesthood; the Need for a New* (7:11). At this point the Preacher switches texts, moving from the Genesis story about Melchizedek to Psalm 110:4, a verse that speaks of "a priest forever after the order of Melchizedek." The Preacher basically argues that the only reason the psalmist would talk about a priesthood of the "order of Melchizedek" is if there were something lacking in the regular order of priests, the Levitical priests, the priesthood of the "order of Aaron." In other words, you don't switch horses in midstream unless the first one is broken down, and you don't get a new priestly order unless there is something wrong with the old one.

The argument here is simple, but the language is loaded. What was wrong with the Levitical priesthood? One could not attain "perfection" through it, and the word "perfection" is not chosen lightly. The Preacher has already told us that Jesus was "made perfect" (see the discussion of the meaning of "perfect" in the comment on 2:10; see also 5:9) and he will soon tell the congregation that they, too, have become "perfected" through Jesus' priestly work (10:14). The Preacher also refers to the "law," and this word is a ticking time bomb as well. The Preacher will soon proclaim that, while Jesus can make us perfect, the law "made nothing perfect" (7:19; see also 7:28; 10:1–10). By "the law," the Preacher is not thinking so much about the law given at Sinai, the Ten Commandments, or the heart of the law, in short, the "law" that Jesus said he came to fulfill (see Matt. 5:17); he is speaking more of the cultic law regarding sacrifices, the law that rests on the Levitical foundation and that "the people received . . . under this priesthood."

D. *A New Law* (7:12). This verse, the last item in this panel of the sermon on the "old" side of the ledger, is actually a transitional statement, allowing the Preacher to move the "old" to the "new." In the previous verse, the Preacher pictured the old sacrificial law resting on the foundation of the old priestly order. Now if you break up the foundation in order to form a new one, whatever was built on the old foundation will necessarily fall. Just so, if we move from the old priestly order, the Levites, to a new one, to Jesus as the great high priest, to Jesus as a "priest forever after the order of Melchizedek," then we are not just changing priests; we are also changing systems of law.

It is to this new priestly order and to the new high priest that the Preacher now turns. The Preacher has listed four claims about the old order (A, B, C, D); he now supplies four matching claims about the new order (A', B', C', D'):

A'. *The Son of God, Who Resembles Melchizedek* (7:13–25). If way back in the midst of the old, God planted a foreshadowing of things to come, namely Melchizedek, who resembled the Son of God (7:3), "in these last days" God has provided a new and greater priest, Jesus, who resembles Melchizedek (7:15).

Jesus was as different from the old priests as day is from night. The old priests were, by law, Levites (see Num. 1:47–54); Jesus, however, was from the tribe of Judah, a clan who never served at the altar and who had no provision in the law of Moses making them priests (7:13–14). The old priests acquired their office through connections, because they had the law on their side and they were born into the right family; Jesus became a priest by virtue of the quality of his life, a life that sin and death could not destroy (7:16).

87

When the old priests assumed office, they did so without taking an oath, but when Jesus became high priest, God took an oath: "The Lord has sworn and will not change his mind, 'You are a priest forever'" (7:20–21; see Ps. 110:4). The Preacher earlier indicated that when God takes an oath it guarantees the steadfastness of what is said (see comment on 6:17–18).

The old priests were mortal, temporary, priests for the time being after the order of Aaron; Jesus was "a priest forever after the order of Melchizedek" (7:17). Because they were mortal, the old priests were "many in number," but there is but one great high priest, one eternal Son.

What are the results of this changing of the guard from the old priesthood to the new? In the first place, the old cultic law as a means to approach God falls away, of course, but that is hardly a loss since that law "made nothing perfect" and was "weak and ineffectual" to begin with (7:18). In its place, we have a new access to God, a highway paved by the priestly labor of Jesus. This highway is more trustworthy, its approach to God more hopeful (7:19), for it is paved on the roadbed of a new and better covenant (7:22; this is the first mention of the new covenant, a reference to Jer. 31:31–24; the preacher will develop this theme in detail in 8:6—9:22).

Moreover, when we send our prayers traveling along that highway to God, when we cry out to God for help in times of need—for mercy, for justice, for confidence, for endurance, for peace—we have a priest who can ably carry those prayers to the throne of God. When we approach God through him, we find him to be a priest who can save completely and for all time (7:25). We do not have a priest who gets sick and dies, or who goes on vacation, or falls down on the job, or grows tired of our need, or compromises his office, or takes advantage of us for his own gain; we have a faithful and steadfast great high priest who can be trusted, who "always lives to make intercession" for us (7:25).

B'. *See How Great Jesus Is!* (7:26—8:6). Earlier, the Preacher called attention to the greatness of Melchizedek because he received tithes even from the patriarch Abraham and blessed him. Now, in a more ecstatic way, the Preacher calls attention to his "main point" (8:1), the greatness of our high priest, Jesus.

See how great he is! The greatness of Jesus can be seen, first of all, because of *who* he is. He slogged it through the muck and mire of human life. He experienced every test, underwent every trial, endured every temptation known to humanity. He bore our griefs and carried our sorrows, and he emerged from it all not beaten and defeated, but steadfast, resolute, "made perfect forever" through suffering (7:28; see 5:9). Because he remained faithful as no other human being has done, he is "holy, blameless, undefiled, separated from sinners and exalted above the heavens" (7:26).

Jesus is great because of the *source of his priestly commission.* Ironically, in terms of the old, earthly priesthood, Jesus would not have qualified for the job. The law required that priests be Levites, and Jesus was of another tribe (see 7:14). So in legal terms Jesus was an "outlaw" priest. But the Preacher's point is that Jesus' priesthood does not rest on the old law but on the eternal will of God. God ordained Jesus; God spoke "the word of the oath" (7:28) that established his ministry.

Jesus is great also because of *where he is.* Ordinary priests perform their ministries in sanctuaries that are but a "sketch and shadow" of the real thing (8:5). Moses was given the blueprints for the earthly sanctuary on Sinai (8:5; see Ex. 25:40), but it was but a copy of the heavenly tabernacle (8:5). Jesus, however, offers his priestly service in the real thing; he is "exalted above the heavens" (7:26) and serves as a minister "in the sanctuary and the true tent that the Lord, and not any mortal, has set up" (8:2).

Jesus' greatness can be seen, as well, in *the offering he brought* as high priest. Every priest must bring an offering to the altar of God. The priests of old brought lambs and bulls, grains and oil. Jesus brought himself. He placed on heaven's altar the deepest possible sacrifice: his own life made perfect through suffering. In other words, he brought as an offering to God nothing less than the fullness of the human condition perfected by his own obedience.

Now when the priests of old made sacrifices, they had to do so every day. Human beings fail every day: faith weakens; resolve breaks down; determination erodes into disobedience. Yesterday's offerings are overwhelmed by today's sins, and the old priests had to trudge back to the sanctuary day after day, a repeated cycle of sin and sacrifice. And these old priests were compelled to this endless daily ritual not only for others, but also for themselves. Appointed under the law, they were themselves weak and sinful (7:28), and the first offerings they placed each day on the altar were for their own transgressions.

But Jesus, the great high priest, does not have to make offerings for himself, and he does not need to make offerings every day. As for himself, unlike the priests of old, he is "without sin" (4:15). He was appointed not by the law but by the oath of God, and God appointed not a sinner but "a Son who has been made perfect forever" (7:28). But what about the rest of us? There is not a day in which we do not fall, not a deed untouched by our weakness, not a moment in which our flawed nature does not shine through. This is true even of those we call "saints," whom one theologian described as "figures out of the Christian past

89

whose lives have been insufficiently researched." Does it not stand to reason that our priest would need to go to the altar for us every day? No, says the Preacher; when Jesus placed himself on the altar of heaven, he was placing not only his own life but also ours, too, offering to God the human condition made perfect through his obedience. Therefore, his sacrifice absolves those transgressions "once for all" (7:27).

Ernest Becker closes his magnificent book *The Denial of Death* by saying that, in the face of life's ambiguities and anguished searchings, "The most that any one of us can seem to do is to fashion something— an object or ourselves—and drop it into the confusion, make an offering of it, so to speak . . ." (p. 285). We want our lives to count for something, to make, in other words, an acceptable offering. But we are plagued by the fear that our offering is finally unacceptable. Not only do we frequently make a mess of our lives, but even when we are at our best, even when we press ourselves to the limit to give and serve and do the right thing, it still seems insufficient. We can never do enough, achieve enough, love enough, give enough, have enough, be noticed enough. Someone is always standing in judgment over us—parents, teachers, employers, strangers, our inner selves—putting us on trial, deeming our efforts to be unacceptable. So day after day we are condemned to trudge to life's altar with a new offering, but it is never satisfactory.

The good news of Jesus' high priestly ministry is that he placed on the heavenly altar, once and for all, not only his life but—astonishingly—ours, too. He gathered up our hunger for approval, and he lived a life truly pleasing to God. He took our restlessness, and brought us to the place of sabbath rest. He carried the human condition and placed it as an offering to God—not the ravaged, broken, humanity that we have made of ourselves, but humanity healed by his own faithfulness, humanity as God intended at the creation, free and joyful, at one with itself, others, and God.

Finally, Jesus is deemed great because of the *benefits of his ministry*. The old priestly order offered sacrifices for sins, but these daily offerings could not fully heal the human heart. Jesus, however, has a "more excellent ministry" (8:6) because his sacrifice fully mends the human spirit; "we have been sanctified through the offering of the body of Jesus Christ once for all" (10:10). The old priests performed their ministries under the cultic law, which to the Preacher's mind is a system of legal rules and requirements that pointed in the right direction but could not finally bring us all the way to the place of rest. Thus the law was only a temporary provision awaiting the coming of a new and better covenant, when the faithful would be less like schoolchildren lockstepping to regulations and more like children at home, with an almost playful freedom and an inner trust of God. Paul once said, "[T]he law was our disciplinarian until Christ came" (Gal. 3:24). The Preacher agrees, and now the ministry of Jesus has inaugurated and mediated that "better covenant" and has embodied those "better promises" of the day when God "will be merciful toward their iniquities and . . . will remember their sin no more" (8:12; see also Jer. 31:34).

C'. Fault with the First Covenant; the Need for a New (8:7–12). Just as the Preacher pointed out how imperfections in the old priestly order required the inauguration of a new order (7:11), he now matches that claim with a similar word about how defects in the old covenant made a new covenant necessary.

When the Preacher speaks of the "first covenant," he means the covenant made between God and Israel at Sinai. After God gave the law through Moses, the people made a solemn vow: "All that the Lord has spoken we will do, and we will be obedient." Then, as a sign of the covenant, Moses dashed the blood of sacrificed oxen on the people and declared, "See the blood of the covenant that the Lord has made with you in accordance with all these words" (see Exod. 24:7–8).

The bad news about the old covenant is that the people broke faith and violated their promises. The first covenant was not an equal affair—God was God, and the people were people—but it was, nonetheless, a two-way arrangement. If the people would hold on firmly to their end of the rope, then God promised to hold on to the other and to pull them to a place of safety and rest. The people vowed that they would, indeed, hold on, but they quickly grew weary and let go. They swore obedience, but, like all human beings, they wavered, buckled, and finally fell (see 3:7–19). No law could make them obey; no ox blood could strengthen their resolve.

The good news, however, is that God did not let go of the rope. The people could not keep faith, but God does. The Preacher's message is that, since the first covenant was not effective, God mercifully makes a better covenant. Because human sin is chronic and tenacious, the old covenant led to a cycle of defeat and despair.

In Saul Bellow's novel *Mr. Sammler's Planet,* Sammler prays for the soul of his good friend, who has just died:

> Remember, God, the soul of Elya Gruner, who, as willingly as possible and as well as he was able, and even to an intolerable point, and even in suffocation and even as death was coming was eager . . . to do what was required of him. . . . He was aware that he must meet, and he did meet—through all the confusion and degraded clowning

91

of this life through which we are speeding—he did meet the terms of his contract. The terms which, in his inmost heart, each man knows. As I know mine. For that is the truth of it—that we all know, God, that we know, we know, we know (p. 313).

The Preacher, though, knows that in the deepest sense none of us is able to "meet the terms of our contract," none of us keeps our holy obligations. Every day we, and the rest of the human race, look into the mirror and know, in our heart of hearts, that we are not living up to our end of any covenant based on obedience to the law. So God established a "new covenant," this time one based on mercy and forgiveness.

The language of "new covenant" comes, of course, from the prophet Jeremiah, specifically Jeremiah 31:31–34, and the Preacher now proceeds to quote that text at length (8:8–12; the quotation is an adaptation of the Septuagint text of Jeremiah). This quotation serves two purposes. Since it describes the failure of Israel "to continue in my covenant" (8:9), it serves as evidence for the Preacher's claim that God found fault with the people and institutions of the first covenant (8:8). It also, however, signifies the transition to the second covenant and names some of the marks of this new covenant, which the Preacher will develop in more detail in chapters 9 and 10. In contrast to the first covenant, the new covenant is an inward reality. The laws of the new covenant are not on the books; they are written on the minds and hearts of the people (8:10). In the new covenant, people do not approach an unknown God; rather, "they shall all know me, from the least of them to the greatest" (8:11). We are not like lost children knocking fearfully on the house of a stranger, but like sons and daughters walking confidently up the path to our own home. Moreover, the new covenant is a bond based on the promise of mercy and forgiveness (8:12); the endless curse of the first covenant, the ceaseless condemnation of never measuring up, of never being worthy, is wiped away in a single gesture of divine kindness and grace.

D'. A New Covenant (8:13). If, as the Preacher said earlier, a change in the priesthood means a change in the law (8:13), that is, a basic shift in the way God relates to human beings, then now, in symmetrical fashion, the Preacher maintains that the establishment of the "new covenant" signals the same sort of turnabout. The new covenant does not lie alongside the old; it replaces it. The whole tragic history of the human race—the sin, the shame, the guilt, the broken promises, the torn relationships—is not the last word; indeed, it is yesterday's news, old, "obsolete," and passing away. The shadows of the long night are rapidly giving way to the brightness of God's new day of mercy.

Priestly Worship, Old and New (9:1–15)

E. *The Old Sanctuary* (9:1–5). In this very inventive passage, the Preacher takes the congregation on a guided tour of the old desert tabernacle, the first sanctuary of Israel under the old covenant (the Preacher's narration is not absolutely precise, but it roughly follows the description of the design and furnishings of the tabernacle woven through Ex. 25—40). The Preacher even takes the congregation where they would not have been allowed to go: into the very inner sanctum, the Holy of Holies.

The old sanctuary was a tent divided by curtains into two chambers, and the Preacher begins the tour by pulling back the flap and inviting the congregation in for a peek at the first chamber. There we see the lampstand (Ex. 25:31–39) and the table with the bread of the Presence (Ex. 25:23–30, see also Mark 2:23–28). Then the tour guide pauses to observe that "We are now in the Holy Place" (9:2).

But there is an even holier place: behind a second curtain is the Holy of Holies, where only the high priest is allowed to go. Suddenly the Preacher causes a gasp by pulling back this curtain, too, and beckoning us to look into its mysterious and forbidden depths. Immediately our eyes are dazzled by gold: the golden incense altar, the ark of the covenant covered with gold. In the ark are the golden jar of manna (Ex. 16:33–34), Aaron's rod (see Num. 17:1–11), and the two tablets of the Decalogue (1 Kings 8:9). On top of the ark is the golden mercy seat with its two pure gold cherubim hovering above (Ex. 25:17–21). In short, gold is everywhere, along with staggering monuments of the covenant. Our imaginations are filled to overflowing.

But then, abruptly, the preacher drops the curtain, and curtly announces that the show is over. "Of these things," he says with a dismissive wave of the hand, "we cannot speak now in detail" (9:5). Why not? Why does the preacher fill our eyes with golden wonders and then bring us to such a precipitate close? In part, he wants to say that the actual details of the old sanctuary, impressive though they be, are beside the point. One could go on and on about lampstands, tables, oil, curtains, vestments, and the like, but the Preacher's main emphasis is on action and meaning, not fixtures and architecture. He wants to contrast what happened—or failed to happen—in the old tabernacle with what happens through the priestly ministry of Jesus.

93

But there is probably another motive as well. The Preacher

knows that the congregation, given a tiny peek at the spellbinding sights in the Holy of Holies, would sigh with disappointment when the curtain rang down. Having glimpsed the treasures of the inner chamber of the sanctuary and having seen the splendors of gold and the riches of the faith, they would want another, longer look. One *National Geographic* photo of Tutankhamen's lavish tomb begs for more. One video clip of the sunken and ghostly *Titanic* teases us to want the cameras to return for a better view. The Preacher is playing peak-a-boo with the congregation, alert to the fact that one glance inside the Holy of Holies will only whet their appetite for more. Eventually, of course, he will take them for a second and better view, not back into the old desert tent, however, but into the "greater and perfect tent" (9:11), into the "heavenly Jerusalem" filled not merely with inanimate objects and statues of cherubim but with real angels, in fact "innumerable angels in festal gathering" (12:22), filled not with stone tablets of the law, but hosts of saints with the law written on their hearts, into the company of a vast congregation of the "righteous made perfect" (12:23). "Just wait," says the Preacher, as he abruptly drops the curtain on the old tabernacle. "You haven't seen anything yet!"

F. *The Actions of the Old Priests* (9:6–10). Having given the congregation a brief tour of the tabernacle, the Preacher now provides an action shot of the old, double-chambered sanctuary at work. First we visit the tabernacle on a routine day. We see typical everyday activity, a stream of busy priests going into the first chamber, the outer tent, to conduct the customary rituals of worship: filling the lamps with oil, freshening the bread of Presence, performing the daily sacrifices (9:6). Next, we see the tabernacle not on an ordinary day but on a very special day, the annual Day of Atonement (see Lev. 16). On this one day during the year the high priest alone goes beyond the outer tent into the second and inner tent, the Holy of Holies, always taking with him, as an offering for his own sins and the sins of the people, a "blood" (that is, animal) sacrifice (9:7).

So on routine days the tabernacle is a beehive of religious ritual; on the one extraordinary Atonement Day, a solitary figure enters the innermost holy place all alone. But why does the Preacher bring this up? He does so because he claims to hear a word from the Holy Spirit in all this (9:8), not just a history lesson, but a "symbol of the present time" (9:9). The Spirit shows the Preacher that this inner-outer tent arrangement is a parable of the theological and pastoral problem this whole sermon is trying to redress.

The Preacher knows that his congregation, like many others, often feels burdened by the toil of the Christian faith but shut out of its joy and peace. Like all other human beings, what the members of the Preacher's congregation really need and want is an encounter with the living God; they want to go into the holiest sanctuary, to have access to God's mercy and forgiveness, but ironically the very rituals of religion block the way. If they are confined to the outer tent of the old tabernacle, if the old system continues to control their religious imaginations and their experience of worship, if they live as if the first covenant were still in effect, they will fiddle with the oil lamps and pour out gallons of energy meeting religious obligations, but they will never get where they need to go. They will be at a deadening committee meeting on the outside, while the living God is in the inner sanctuary.

In her book *The Preaching Life*, Barbara Brown Taylor tells of her days as the coordinator for Christian education for a parish church. People in the congregation repeatedly told her how hungry they were for Bible study. So, in response to their expression of need, she frequently hired professors from a nearby seminary to teach courses on the Old and New Testaments. When people saw the course announcements, they said they looked good, but, strangely, attendance was always poor. Nevertheless, even though people did not come to the classes, every quarter they continued to ask for more Bible. So she provided more, and still people stayed away.

"Finally," she writes, "I got the message. 'Bible' was a code word for 'God.' People were not hungry for information about the Bible; they were hungry for an experience of God, which the Bible seemed to offer them." From then on, she began to offer a different kind of Bible study, a kind that moved beyond information about the biblical text to encounter with God through the text; attendance soared (Taylor, p. 47).

That is precisely what the Preacher is talking about. People want God, but instead they often get information about God. People hunger for transcendence, but as a substitute they frequently get a religion of rules, procedures, and preliminaries. People are trapped in the vestibule, and they cannot get inside the sanctuary. They are busy, very busy, put to work studying the Bible, observing regulations about "food and drink" (9:10), organizing prayer chains and trips to the Holy Land, keeping rules "for the body" (9:10), planning the stewardship campaign, and generally laboring hard at the business of being religious. None of this activity is evil; indeed, most of it is good and useful, but it is not the thing itself, the thing we seek—access to the living and healing God.

This problem with a religion that is confined to the outer tent, a religion that bustles with activity but lacks real holy encounter, is that

95

people finally grow weary and lose hope. So much hard work, so little real worship. So much struggle and toil, so little Sabbath rest. The Preacher sees this plight represented in the old tabernacle, the old priesthood, the old covenant; this is, in fact, the "symbol of the present time" that the Spirit reveals to the Preacher. The whole old scheme shouts of unbearable burdens, inadequacy, and imperfection. Everybody hungers for access to the holy, but under the old regime only the high priest could go in; everybody needs God's mercy and help every day, but the high priest could approach the holy but once a year; humanity thirsts for freedom from guilt, a fresh start, a healed spirit, but the blood sacrifices of the old high priest could not "perfect the conscience of the worshiper" (9:9).

In other words, if there is to be true atonement, then what went on inside that tiny back room of the tabernacle once a year with an elite congregation of one and in an imperfect fashion needs to happen in the spaciousness of the cosmos, once for all, for the whole of humanity, and with a perfect and efficacious sacrifice. If so, we will need a new high priest and a new covenant and a new law and a new and open sanctuary. We will need a high priest who will offer a sacrifice that is genuinely acceptable. We will need a high priest who is not a frightened sinner, but a Son, an heir, one who is at home in the Holy of Holies and who can boldly and permanently pull back the great curtain that shuts us out from God and can invite us all, as brothers and sisters, to come in, to enter into intimacy with the living God.

The good news of the gospel, says the Preacher, is that this is precisely the high priest we have.

The previous two sections (E and F) of this miniature sermon are now paired with matching sections describing the new covenant (E' and F'):

E'. *The "Greater and Perfect" New Sanctuary* (9:11). Under the first covenant, the old priests moved through a temporary tent made of skins and cloth to place their offerings on a humanly crafted mercy seat. But when the new covenant of mercy and forgiveness came to sweep away the old, Jesus Christ, the high priest of these "good things that have come" (9:11), moved through the heavens (4:14), "through the greater and perfect tent" not humanly crafted (9:11), to present his offering to the living God.

The point of all this is not so much about geography—the idea that Jesus traveled through the clouds to place an offering on the heavenly altar—but about the passing away of everything regarding worship that is temporary, provisional, and imperfect. Christians worship on Sunday morning, or Saturday afternoon, or Wednesday evening. They worship in tiny wooden frame chapels, or cavernous cathedrals, or in a circle of chairs drawn up in the front room of an apartment. Regardless of the place, everything seems time-bound and contingent. The seasons change; the pews creak; people come and go; congregations rise and fall; neighborhoods change; buildings crumble; the photographs on the walls bear witness to the passing of the generations and the transience of human life. Nevertheless, proclaims the Preacher, whenever and wherever the Christian community gathers for worship, it follows its great high priest into "the greater and perfect tent"—into a sanctuary that will not decay—to join in a fellowship that will not perish and sing hymns of praise that will not cease to a God whose mercy is everlasting.

F'. *The Actions of the New High Priest* (9:12–15). This section employs a "how much more" style of argument to contrast the actions of the old priests with that of Christ. The old priests sacrificed animals— goats and calves, bulls and heifers (see Lev. 16:5–15; Num. 19:1–10)— and the Preacher acknowledges that these old sacrifices and the purification rituals that accompanied them were to a certain extent effective. They at least gave people the kind of external purity that allowed them to operate in the community and to participate in worship, what the Preacher calls purifications of the "flesh" (9:13). They anticipated what was to come, but could not achieve it.

But Jesus, the great high priest, offered not an animal but himself, a sacrifice truly "without blemish" (9:14). If the old sacrifices were valid in their own limited way, how much more will this perfect sacrifice be effective to restore human life to what God intended it to be. The old sacrifices provided a provisional and transient release from ritual impurity; the sacrifice of Jesus provides lasting, "eternal redemption" (9:12). The old sacrifices furnished outer purity; the sacrifice of Jesus purifies the inner person, the "conscience," freeing the faithful from "dead works," toilsome and futile attempts to make peace with God on their own, and opening the way to authentic and intimate worship of the living God (9:14).

As Jesus said to the Samaritan woman at Jacob's well, "The hour is coming, and is now here, when the true worshipers will worship the Father in spirit and in truth, for the Father seeks such as these to worship him" (John 4:23). The Preacher tells the congregation that this worship in spirit and in truth, this worship for which all human beings hunger, is made possible by the perfect sacrifice of Christ.

For this reason Jesus is called "the mediator of a new covenant." This new covenant is a rainbow sign of the generosity of God, the eternal kindness of a God who will not leave humanity weary and spent and

97

without hope, the divine kindness that rolls back through time to refresh all of God's children in every age. Here the Preacher shows his deepest theological understanding regarding the people of the Old Testament. They were people who clung to the promises of God even when they could not see how these promises would be fulfilled. They were, then, people in waiting, people on a journey toward a land they could not yet see, and everything about their approach to God carried the symbolism of the transitory. They offered imperfect sacrifices through flawed priests in a temporary and movable tabernacle that screened them from the holy presence, but all of this was straining ahead toward the "good things" that were to come.

They were reaching forward toward a God they could not grasp, and now God has reached back to take their hands. They were children of the promises toiling under the old covenant, and now the God who made those promises keeps them. Because of the death of Jesus, the link to the living God they were straining toward and hoping for but could not themselves forge has been given as a gift. They have received "the promised eternal inheritance" and been redeemed "from the transgressions under the first covenant" (9:15). The Christ-event has not replaced the Old Testament promises, and the church has not replaced the people of Israel. The people of God from beginning to end form a great chain of faith. Those under the old covenant were the first links, but only the first links, in a long chain. With only these first links the chain was incomplete, so it was attached to those who come after. But a chain, no matter how long, must finally be fastened to something or it simply drops. The Preacher claims that Jesus took the end of the chain and anchored it in the Holy Place (see 6:19). In Christ all the promises of old have been brought to completion, and all that the faithful hoped for under the old covenant has been realized (see "Excursus: Hebrews and Judaism," p. 12).

Death and Purification (9:16–28)

The mention of death in the previous passage (9:15) provides the segue into this next section of the sermon-within-a-sermon, in which the Preacher develops the complex theological idea that purification requires a blood sacrifice. Again, he follows the usual pattern of contrasting the old (section G) with the new (section G').

G. *Purification through Death: Old Covenant* (9:16–22). The Preacher begins the section with a pun and an analogy. The pun is on the word "covenant," which can also mean "testament" or "will." For two chapters the Preacher has been talking about "covenant," the old

98

one and the new, and now, through a little wordplay, he transforms "covenant" into "will." A will only takes effect, he observes, when the person who made the will dies (9:17). In other words, a will is just a piece of paper, null and void, until there is a death.

Just so, claims the Preacher, a covenant is nothing until there is a death; this was true even of the first covenant, and it is certainly true of the new covenant. At Sinai, the first covenant was inaugurated by what amounted to a death ritual as Moses sprinkled animal blood on the scroll, the tent, the implements of worship, and all the people, saying, "This is the blood of the covenant that God has ordained for you" (9:18–21; see Ex. 24:3–8). Under the law that backs up that first covenant, almost every purification ritual demands death, sacrifice, the use of blood (9:22).

To clench his point that covenant and death are inextricably linked, the Preacher cites a saying well-known in ancient literature and probably familiar to the congregation: "Without the shedding of blood there is no forgiveness of sins" (9:22). It would be a mistake to hold this statement too tightly, since the Preacher is not formulating dogma or coming to some new theological insight here as much as he is rounding out this section with a traditional quotation, something like, "And as we all know, 'No shedding of blood, no forgiveness. . . .'"

Moreover, taken as a strict doctrinal principle, this statement is simply not true; there are plenty of examples in Scripture of forgiveness, both human and divine, that happen without a death being involved. What the Preacher is doing here is spinning wisdom, citing a far more profound version of another maxim: "If you want to make a cake, you have to break eggs." If you want a covenant, it comes with a price. Forgiveness is not cheap or easy; it costs. Ultimately, the forgiveness of human beings, the great mercy of the new covenant, came with a grave cost: the death of Jesus the Son. When the last will and testament is read, the brothers and sisters of Jesus "receive the promised eternal inheritance" (9:15), but "where a will is involved, the death of the one who made it must be established" (9:16).

G'. *Purification through the Death of Christ* (9:23–28). Having described how the old covenant was inaugurated with animal sacrifice, the Preacher next moves over to the "new" side of the ledger. Under the old covenant, worship was not the real thing; it was an imitation of heavenly worship (the "sketches of the heavenly things"—9:23). Even so, it required sacrifice, the blood of animals. How much more, then, will "the heavenly things themselves" (9:23), *real* worship, need even better sacrifices.

It was, of course, Jesus Christ who provided these "better sacrifices," and in describing them the Preacher repeats many of the themes he has already developed. Once more we hear that Christ did not go into a desert tent of human construction, but into heaven itself (9:24; see 9:11). Once more we hear that, unlike the old high priest who had to go back into the tent over and over, year after year, Jesus made a final and fitting sacrifice once. Jesus is not condemned to an eternity of crucifixions, a ceaseless round of suffering, a never-ending and always unfinished series of little atonements. No, the work of redemption is done, finished, complete; as the old hymn says, "The strife is o'er, the battle done, the victory of life is won; the song of triumph has begun. Alleluia!" Jesus was offered once, and it was sufficient to "save many" (9:25–28; see 7:27–28).

We have heard all this before. The Preacher is basically circling back for another view of scenery we have already surveyed. One new and surprising feature, however, appears on the landscape: the announcement that Christ "will appear a second time" (9:28). Contrary to those doleful preachers who conjure up a picture of a wrathful and punitive Jesus coming back to kick sinners and take names ("You better watch out, you better not cry, you better not pout, I'm telling you why. Jesus Christ is coming again!"), the Preacher of Hebrews knows that Jesus' return is good news indeed.

He conveys this good news by citing a piece of commonsense wisdom: "Everybody dies once, and then comes the judgment." When the Preacher says this, the first reaction of the congregation is probably no reaction. The concept of death followed by judgment was so conventional and universally held that the congregation would barely notice it, much less challenge it. Something like this was frequently preached in churches and synagogues, and it was routinely accepted by the Greeks, too. Plato preached it; Plutarch preached it; people today routinely accept it. "Everybody dies, and then you meet your Maker." That's the way it is; nobody has a monopoly on this idea.

In fact, when the Preacher said it, it seemed as though he was using it matter-of-factly as an analogy. He seemed to be making the obvious point that, just as ordinary humans die only once, just so Jesus died only once, too. He did not have to repeat his sacrifice but died on the cross one time. But then the Preacher extends this truth in a surprising way. For those who hold on to his priestly ministry, Jesus has overthrown this pattern of death followed by judgment (here judgment is taken in the fearsome and punitive sense, not in the more positive sense of coming to establish justice; for an example of judgment taken positively, see 2 Thess. 1:5). What happened in Jesus' death was that the power of sin was defeated. He has borne the "sins of many"; he has taken into himself the judgment. Therefore he is coming back not to punish but to rescue his own. Because of the sufficiency of his death, the perfection of his sacrifice, he does not have to come back to "deal with sin" (9:28), to pump out the cesspools of iniquity and to torment sinners; sin has already been vanquished. He comes instead to gather his brothers and sisters, those who do not fear his coming but who trust him and "who are eagerly waiting for him" (9:28), and to take them home. He comes not as wrathful judge, but as savior. No longer is it true that "It is appointed that a human being dies once and faces the judgment." Now the truth is, "It is appointed by God that Jesus died once for all, and then comes the saving mercy."

The Benefits of the
Priestly Ministry (10:1–18)

Again in this section the Preacher seems to be running his homiletical harrow over already plowed ground. All of the themes here are familiar—the unfinished nature of the old sacrifices versus the perfection of the new, inwardness of the new covenant, the once-for-all character of the atonement that comes through Christ. In fact, in terms of content there are no new arguments here, only a few fresh nuances, and the basic purpose of this section is to sum up this sermon-within-a-sermon. In terms of rhetorical impact, however, there is something new. The Preacher is driving home the central claim of the sermon, and one could think of this section as a repeated assurance of pardon: "In Jesus Christ you are forgiven; in Jesus Christ you are forgiven; in Jesus Christ, I tell you, you are forgiven."

H. *The Old, Repeated Sacrifices* (10:1–4). The Preacher keeps to his customary design: he talks about the old covenant side of the ledger (section H), and then he moves over to the new (section H'). The problem, he says, with the sacrifices in the old cult, offered under the law, is that they leave the people inwardly guilty. If they were effective to cleanse people from sin and to make them perfect in the sight of God, then they would not come back year after year to offer the same sacrifices. In short, the sacrifices of the old covenant may ritually cleanse the surface, but people are still left with a guilty conscience (10:2). In fact, the whole Day of Atonement ritual, repeated annually, is like a sledgehammer to the human spirit, pounding away year after year after year with its constant battering away on the theme of sin. In other words, it does not work to heal; it works only to drub it into us that we are sinful, sinful, sinful—guilty, and unacceptable to God.

Most contemporary Christians do not, of course, observe the Day of Atonement, but many know the underlying reality the Preacher

101

describes. Often churches are far more effective in preaching sin than they are in proclaiming grace. Sunday after Sunday, month after month, year after year, sermon after sermon beats out the message of sin. Every Sunday is the "Day of Atonement," but sadly an atonement we must accomplish for ourselves. The sacrifices placed on the altar are those of the unfortunate congregation who have come to be told one more time that they do not measure up and, because this is the constant theme, become convinced they will never measure up. Listen, for example, to one woman, fighting a lifelong battle with psychological depression, as she describes the message she heard in church:

> In the "badness" of my childhood depression, I was teeth-rattlingly lonely. . . . The . . . Christianity of my childhood offered me no way out of my unhappiness. Rather, with its emphasis on sin, on the thorough badness of all people, and Jesus' death for it, it gave me an explanation for why I ought to be depressed. Sin was what religion was about. If you had asked me in the fourth grade, "Why was Jesus born?" I would have been glad to answer, "It was because of sin. . . ." If you had pushed me about what it took to get our sins forgiven, I would have told you, "We have to repent of our sins." If you had pushed me a little further to ask, "And what does it mean to repent?" I would have said, "To feel really, really bad about what a sinful person you are" (Bondi, pp. 153–54).

H'. *The "Once for All" Sacrifice of Christ* (10:5–18). The old, law-based pattern of religion, whether it occurs in the ancient desert tabernacle or in First Church on Main Street, condemns people to come to worship time and again with a guilty conscience. We try to absolve our guilt by bringing sacrifices with us; repeatedly we bring sacrifices—"Lord, didn't I give of myself generously to serve as an advisor for the youth group?"; "Lord, didn't you hear me pray for the sick in our church?"; "Lord, didn't you notice how I stood up for minority hiring in my company?"; "Lord, at least I come to church; many do not, you know"; "Lord, I know I'm not perfect, but I do the best I can. Doesn't it count Lord? Doesn't it count?" Over and over we make these offerings, but it does not work. It is never enough, never adequate; so we keep our distance from the Holy of Holies, leave with a guilty conscience, and come back next week with another basket of good intentions and deeds to place on the altar—or we stay away altogether.

Therefore, the Preacher employs yet another text from the Old Testament, a quotation from Psalm 40, to relate the good news that the never-ending cycle of guilt sacrifices is over, that when "Christ came into the world, he spoke to God and said, 'Sacrifices you do not want; sin offerings give you no pleasure. What you do want, O God, is for your will to be done. Here I am, O God. I have come to do your will'"

(10:5–7; see Ps. 40:6–8). And Jesus, though he was tested in every way as we are, remained obedient and faithful. Then he placed his own faithful life on the altar on behalf of us all, and it was enough. "It is by God's will," says the Preacher, "that we have been sanctified through the offering of the body of Jesus Christ once for all" (10:10). "I tell you: In the name of Jesus Christ you are forgiven."

Then the Preacher begins to sing this point home. What endless and repeated priestly sacrifices could not do, he hymns, Jesus accomplished with "a single sacrifice" (10:12). Having finished his work, he took his seat, the seat of authority "at the right hand of God" (10:12). The war has been won, and now the mopping up is taking place. The victorious Son is waiting for all of his enemies, all of the manifestations of sin—disease, poverty, warfare, hunger, loneliness, anger, despair . . . even the final enemy, death—to "be made a footstool for his feet" (10:13; see Ps. 110:1). He has established the new covenant, a covenant where God says "I will put my laws in their hearts and write them on their minds" (10:16; see Jer. 31:33).

And then the Preacher comes to the theological climax of the whole sermon-within-the-sermon. Everything he has been proclaiming since 7:1 now comes to laser focus. Because of the ministry of our great high priest, "holy, blameless, undefiled" (7:26), the curtain shielding the Holy of Holies has been parted, and the way to the living God has been opened. We can approach with confidence because the merciful voice of God announces, "I will remember their sins and their lawless deeds no more."

"I tell you: In the name of Jesus Christ you are forgiven."

Earlier, the Preacher quoted a well-known saying: "Without the shedding of blood there is no forgiveness of sins." In other words: no costly sacrifice, no forgiveness. But Jesus, the great high priest, has made the unblemished offering, the sacrifice of himself on behalf of all, and he has "perfected for all time those who are sanctified." So, pick up your bed and walk. Rise and put oil on your face. Your warfare is ended; your iniquity is pardoned. Because of what Jesus accomplished, never again do we have to say of ourselves, "Without the shedding of blood there is no forgiveness." What we are free to say is, "Where there is forgiveness, there is no longer any sacrifice," no longer any shedding of blood. "I tell you: In the name of Jesus Christ you are forgiven."

The Worship of the New Covenant (10:19–39)

I′. Getting Ready to Go to Worship (10:19–25). Every sermon implies a "so what?" and this sermon-within-a-sermon is no exception.

The Preacher has just taken the congregation through a long christo-logical journey spanning three-and-one-half chapters. Now he must answer the implied question that hangs in their minds, "If what you have said is true, what shall we do in response?"

The answer? Get ready for worship. The high priestly ministry of Jesus has made it possible genuinely to worship—not just to sit in the pew and go through the motions, but truly to have access to the Holy Place, to be brought into communion with the merciful and generous God of all the Ages. In the days of the former covenant, the old high priest—and no one else—parted the curtain and entered into the tent called the "Holy of Holies." Under the new covenant, however, all of God's children enter into the Holy of Holies. The great high priest Jesus, through his death (his "flesh"), has opened up a "new and living way" into the true sanctuary and beckoned us to come in with him (10:19).

As we have seen, the undergirding structure of the Preacher's christology is what we have called the "parabola of salvation" (see comments on 1:5–14). Jesus the Son moved down into human history, experienced testing and suffering of every kind, and then swept back up into the heavenly places. Now the Preacher proclaims that this parabolic arc was not only the pathway that Christ traveled, it is also a pilgrim way of grace that we travel, a highway leading into the very presence of God opened up by the ministry of Jesus the great high priest:

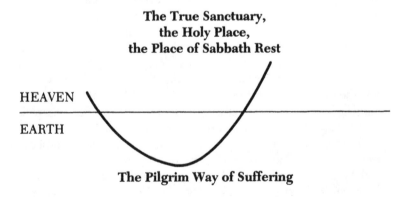

The True Sanctuary,
the Holy Place,
the Place of Sabbath Rest

HEAVEN

EARTH

The Pilgrim Way of Suffering

Figure 5

How shall we travel this pilgrim path toward the true sanctuary? How shall we prepare ourselves to enter into the presence of the living God? How, in other words, do we get ready for authentic worship?

1. We go to worship *as a community*. The opening words of this

section, "therefore brothers and sisters" (NRSV = "friends"; 10:19), are a sign that we travel to the place of true worship together, as brothers and sisters, belonging both to each other and to Jesus (see 2:11). We are no longer strangers and outcasts, relegated to the outer tent; we are family, kin, welcomed into the inner rooms of the house of God.

In fact, the first thing we are to do is to come boldly into the house of God as those who belong to the family. "We have confidence to enter the sanctuary," the Preacher says (10:19). As brothers and sisters of Jesus Christ, we are welcomed into the place the human heart longs to be, in the very presence of God. The old covenant left us with perpetual guilt, but the new covenant is one of grace, and grace, as the familiar hymn has it, "will lead me home."

Jonathan Kozol's book *Amazing Grace* borrows its title from that old hymn. It is a narrative study of the lives of children in the South Bronx, the poorest congressional district in the United States. One of the people described in this book is Anthony, a twelve-year-old boy who has been exposed to more street violence, crime, and poverty than a young life ought to endure, but who has also experienced the tender ministries of a local church. When Kozol noticed that Anthony often spoke of "the kingdom of God," he asked Anthony to write a description of what he meant by such language. At first the boy resisted the suggestion, but a few days later he showed Kozol three pages in his spiral notebook titled "God's Kingdom." There, among other things, Anthony had written:

> No violence will be in heaven. There will be no guns or drugs or IRS. You won't have to pay taxes. You'll recognize all the children who have died when they were little. Jesus will be good to them and play with them. At night he'll come and visit at your house (Kozol, *Amazing Grace*, p. 238).

The Preacher would nod assent to Anthony's description. The Son who sits in majesty is no distant deity but our brother, and we "are no more a stranger or a guest, but like a child at home."

2. We also come to worship as those who are *baptized and forgiven*. We come to the "house of God" (10:21; see 3:1–6) through the gate of baptism, with "our bodies washed with pure water" (10:22). This outer purification, however, is but the sign that God has provided a deeper, inner cleansing so that we can approach God "with a true heart in full assurance of faith" (10:22). We come, then, reassured of God's acceptance. Though we spend our lives in sometimes half-hearted commitments, heartsick over the brokenness in our lives, and with hearts heavy-laden by the cares of life, in worship the "heart

105

disease" of humanity is touched by God's forgiveness and cured, "sprinkled clean" by the grace of God (10:22; see 9:13–15).

3. We come *hoping and holding on to the promises of God.* God has promised that a day is coming when war will be ended, when justice will flow down like a waterfall, and when death and pain will be no more. God has promised that a time is coming when no mother will weep again for her lost children, when all will have a place to live and food to eat, when many will come from east and west, north and south for a great homecoming at God's extravagant banquet table. But Christians must live in a world where "we do not yet see" the realization of these promises (2:8); therefore, Christians must live by hope. They must "hold fast to the confession of our hope without wavering" (10:23). "Christian faith," writes theologian Daniel Migliore, "is expectant faith. It eagerly awaits the completion of the creative and redemptive activity of God" (Migliore, *Faith Seeking Understanding*, p. 231).

The Preacher thinks of hope almost literally as a strong cord—an unbreakable cable—linking us, who are in the middle of the struggle, to the firm and sure promises of God. As a physician working in an AIDS clinic, who gets up every morning to find the wards more crowded and the statistics in disheartening free-fall, said, "I am clinging to my faith; I am clinging to the possibility of hope." Christians do not claim to know how or when God's promises will be fulfilled, but they hold on for dear life to the confession, to the bold affirmation of the Nicene Creed that "we look for the resurrection of the dead, and the life of the world to come." As theologian Douglas John Hall maintains, "While faith leaves to God the 'how' of such a consummation, it is never silent about the 'what' and the 'why' of it. [Christians profess] their faith in a God who wills to complete and fulfill the promises of a creation that has been visited and redeemed by the love that made it" (Hall, *Professing the Faith*, p. 359).

When we "hold fast to the confession of our hope," we are doing far more than holding on to a doctrine or an abstract idea; we are holding on to the One who gives us hope, Jesus Christ. To "hold fast," then, is to say, in the words of the gospel song, "Hear my cry, hear my call, hold my hand lest I fall; take my hand, precious Lord, lead me home."

4. When we come to worship, we come not just to pray and sing, but also praising God *with deeds of compassion and mercy.* In fact, since our bent is to leave "undone those things we ought to have done," we are to be aggressive, prodding each other to works of mercy. "Consider how to provoke one another to love and good deeds," says the Preacher (10:24). On the rare occasions today when church discipline is exercised, it is usually understood as correcting someone who has

106

gone astray, who has done something wrong. The Preacher, however, instead of the idea of pulling people back from the wrong path, suggests a notion of church discipline as pushing each other along on the right path.

5. Perhaps surprisingly, we come to the true and heavenly sanctuary to engage in pure and eternal worship by *gathering with other Christians* in ordinary sanctuaries for prayers and hymns, preaching and blessings. Whether it is high mass or prayer meeting, a eucharist or a revival, choral evensong with a boys' choir or a praise service with a synthesizer; whether it takes place in St. Peter's Basilica on Christmas Eve, Macedonia Baptist on Sunday night, or in the coffee room of the office on Thursday morning before work, whenever Christians cluster together for worship we walk through the doorway of an ordinary building, an "earthly tent," and find ourselves in the company of heaven singing praises with the heavenly hosts.

In other words, Christian worship is an eschatological event; it is a participation here and now in the eternal praises of God, a foretaste of the approaching victory of God. A time is coming, wrote Paul, when "every knee should bend on heaven and in earth and every tongue should confess that Jesus Christ is Lord to the glory of God the Father" (Phil. 2:10–11). Now the knees that bend and the tongues that confess are serving as midwives of the future of God, always with an eye on "the Day approaching" (10:25). As the words of the familiar hymn state, "O that with yonder sacred throng, we at his feet may fall! We'll join the everlasting song, and crown him Lord of all!"

Garret Keizer has written a beautiful and telling description of his work as a lay minister in a small Episcopal church in Vermont. He describes a Saturday night Easter vigil service at which only he and two other people were present. He began the service by lighting the Paschal candle and praying, "O God . . . grant in this Paschal feast we may so burn with heavenly desires, that with pure minds we may attain to the festival of everlasting light." As he prays, he is struck by the ambiguity of the situation:

> The candle sputters in the half darkness, like a voice too embarrassed or overwhelmed to proclaim the news: "Christ is risen." But it catches fire, and there we are, three people and a flickering light— in an old church, on a Saturday evening. . . . The moment is filled with the ambiguities of all such quiet observances among few people, in the midst of an oblivious population in a radically secular age. The act is so ambiguous because its terms are so extreme; the Lord is with us, or we are pathetic fools (Keizer, *A Dresser of Sycamore Trees*, p. 73).

107

It is easy, of course, to lose sight of that, to let go of the truth that the little company gathered in a local congregation are gathered up into presence of the Lord and the great company of the saints, and thus it is hard to maintain the practice of worshiping together. The Preacher knew, and points out that, frankly, attendance at services had not been all that it could be. Some had gotten into the "habit," he notes, of "neglecting to meet together" (10:25), and we can understand that. The disincentives to corporate worship are many. It seems somehow purer to worship God all alone on a deserted beach or in the still beauty of the night under the canopy of stars rather than in the midst of the ragtag assembly that shows up for church.

Also, we just get tired, tired in worship and tired of worship. It is not only that the sermon may ramble on for a tad too long or that the pace of the service can sometimes lag; the weariness of worship is a deeper fatigue, a jaded sense that nothing of real significance happens here. The local video store has better drama; television has more interesting stories; the pool club has friendlier people; the park has a nicer view; the Sunday paper has more intrigue, and sleeping in provides a more profound Sabbath rest. What is more, nobody at the beach or the backyard barbecue is going to hand us a pledge card, call us to pray for people in a country whose name we cannot pronounce, or ask us to teach the junior high youth.

The only thing about that, says the Preacher, is that while we are in the beach chair filling out the crossword puzzle, the faithful in the sanctuary, doing the best they can with their off-key voices to belt out "Holy, Holy, Holy," have been gathered by a mystery beyond their own seeing and knowing into the great choir of the angels in festal garb and the saints singing ceaseless praises to God (12:22–23). Things are not what they seem. What looks like leisure turns out in the end to be exhausting, and what appears to be the labor of prayer leads to "a safe lodging, and a holy rest, and peace at the last."

J'. *Warnings and Encouragement* (10:26–39). Somewhat startlingly, the Preacher's mood now becomes stern. After nearly four chapters lyrically describing how the high priestly ministry of Jesus Christ cleanses us from sin and brings us, free and forgiven, into the joyful presence of God, thunderclouds now gather in the sermon and the lightning bolts of judgment begin to flash.

The Preacher has proclaimed the gospel truth about the ministry of Jesus Christ on our behalf, but here he issues a grim warning. "If we willfully persist in sin after having received the knowledge of the truth," he says, "there no longer remains a sacrifice for sins but a fearful prospect of judgment" (10:26–27). These are terrifying words, es-

108

pecially since we know that no Christian is perfect; the most faithful still to some degree "persist in sin."

In order to move toward understanding this difficult passage, several factors are important:

First, in this text the concept of sin has a very specific focus. When the Preacher speaks of willful persistence in sin, he is not here talking about sin in the Pauline sense as the human condition, the chronic situation of knowing the right thing to do but never being able to do it. When sin is taken in this more pervasive sense, the Preacher shares Paul's cry, "Wretched man that I am! Who will rescue me from this body of death? Thanks be to God through Jesus Christ our Lord!" (Rom. 7:24–25; see Heb. 9:14, 28; 10:10).

In this passage, though, sin is very specifically apostasy: the clear, firm, informed, and deliberate rejection of the gospel by those who have already lived in its joy, who have felt its purifying power, and who know in the marrow of their souls the promises of God and the grace God offers (10:29).

For those who willfully turn away from grace, there is the "fearful prospect of judgment." The Preacher quotes scripture to say that vengeance belongs to God and that the "Lord will judge his people" (10:30; see Deut. 32:35–36). We must be careful not to hear such language through the mouthpiece of a thousand petulant hellfire and brimstone sermons. In the Scripture, the judgment of God is good news, a sign that God's love for the world will allow nothing to stand that will harm or destroy. The idea of judgment does not convey a picture of a peevish God who gets mad at sinners and strikes out in retaliation; rather, God exercises "good judgment." God's judgment sets things right, repairs the broken creation.

"The glory of God," said Irenaeus, "is humanity fully alive," and what God judges are all those forces that destroy human life and tear at the fabric of the creation. Ultimately, then, what God judges is death, and "the sting of death is sin" (1 Cor. 15:56). It is a wonderful grace to rest in the hand of the living and saving God, unless, of course, one decides to join forces with death. Only for servants of death is it "a fearful thing to fall into the hands of the living God" (10:31).

Apostasy is to know in the depth of one's soul that "death has been swallowed up in victory" (1 Cor. 15:54) but to choose nonetheless to pitch one's tent in a death camp. Apostasy is to know full well where the next earthquake will be and to leave "a kingdom that cannot be shaken" (12:28) to build one's life on the fault line. Apostasy is to have been a child in heavenly Jerusalem's palace but to choose to leave home in order to be a slave in Sodom. Apostasy is to have been drawn

109

by a strong cord into the lifeboat and then to jump back into the raging sea. In the case of apostasy, sin has tragic proportions, and judgment is woven into the fabric of the choice.

Second, as we saw in an earlier section of the sermon (see commentary on 6:1–8), the Preacher is addressing a very practical and urgent pastoral problem. Apostasy, abandonment of the gospel and the community of faith, is not a hypothetical possibility; it is an everyday threat. The Preacher's congregation is like a group of imperiled rock climbers who are being pulled to safety by the rope of faith. Just as they are nearing the top of the rock face, they have decided that they are growing tired and they just might let go of the rope. No wonder the Preacher screams out a warning, "If you let go there is no saving you!"

To turn up the volume on the urgency, the Preacher compares judgment under the old covenant with judgment under the new, making a similar analogy to one he used before (see 2:1–4). Under the old covenant, anyone who engages in a wholesale rejection of the law of Moses "dies without mercy" (10:28). All it takes is "the testimony of two or three witnesses" (see Deut. 19:15). If such dire punishment under the old covenant was certain, goes the argument, how much more will there be sad consequences for those who turn their backs on great promises of the new covenant.

Third, just as was the case with the earlier pastoral warning (see comments on 6:1–8 and 6:9–12), the Preacher's real goal is to generate not fear but encouragement. He wants the faithful in his congregation to keep their "eyes on the prize," not to forfeit the great reward that comes to those who, like their Lord, endure the trials with hope and compassion.

The move toward encouragement begins when the Preacher prompts them to remember a piece of their own congregational history. In their "earlier days," probably quite soon after they had responded to the preaching of the gospel and become part of the Christian movement ("after you had been enlightened"), they had experienced some form of persecution (10:32). It is not possible to recover precise details, but it evidently involved verbal insults (sometimes in public), the loss of personal possessions, and a measure of physical abuse, though not to the point of death (10:33–34; see 12:4). Whatever the nature of this "hard struggle," it was not confined to the Preacher's congregation but had spread to other Christians as well ("partners"), some of whom had been imprisoned (10:33–34).

110 What is the Preacher referring to here? Was the congregation on the outer curl of one of those waves of Roman persecution that rippled through the early church? Or is the Preacher speaking of a more local

chain of events, the sort of neighborhood hassling that even today in some places greets new converts, exposing them to rejection and disownment from their shame-filled families and villages? Theories abound, but we simply do not know.

What we do know, however, is how the congregation responded to this earlier crisis: with compassion and joy. The imprisonment of others became not an occasion for despair but for the formation of a prison ministry (10:34). The loss of possessions did not prompt them to cry, "We've lost everything!" but, "We possess a treasure the world cannot take" (10:34). In other words, the congregation sang no dismal songs of victimhood but a triumphant hymn of praise: "Let goods and kindred go. This mortal life also; The body they may kill, God's truth abideth still; His kingdom is forever."

It is precisely that kind of confident faith, says the Preacher, that the congregation needs to preserve (10:35). To bring his point home, to provide a rousing close to this sermon-within-a-sermon that has been uncoiling since 7:1, and to anticipate the issue he wants to address in the next section of Hebrews, the Preacher does what many preachers after him have done: he borrows an image from the wide world of sports. He actually smuggled it into the sermon at 10:32, since the phrase "you endured a hard struggle with suffering" employs an athletic metaphor and can more literally be translated "you endured a contest of suffering."

Notice what this subtle sports image accomplishes: it refashions their experience of persecution. What looks for all the world like an experience of abuse and mistreatment, public humiliation and plundering, turns out, from the perspective of faith, to be a "contest," an Olympic time trial. This also redefines the word "endurance," moving it from a negative experience ("Look what you had to endure") to an athletic virtue ("For you need endurance," 10:36), transforming it from a bitter description of the abuse they had to stomach to a naming of the strength and conditioning in faith they received as a result of staying out there on the field.

The Preacher knows that his congregation is tired, discouraged, and playing with injuries. The danger is that they will lose perspective and forget who they are, where they are, and the nature of the event, and simply quit. Losing sight of the goal, they will fear that they are merely running ragged rather than running in the great marathon of all time (see 12:1). So the Preacher tells them what they cannot see: you are running in the supreme contest of humanity; the end of the race is near, and the victor's prize of the "promised eternal inheritance" awaits (10:36; see 9:15).

111

Every athlete needs to hear shouts of encouragement from the stands, and the Preacher summons cheerleading from no less than the prophets Isaiah and Habakkuk. Blending a loose translation of Habakkuk 2:3–4 with a few words from Isaiah 26:20, the Preacher allows these voices from the Old Testament to spur on the runners on the track. As presented by the Preacher these prophets of old say, in effect, "Do not hold back. The time left is very short, so push on, harder, harder" (10:37–38).

The Preacher knows his congregation, and he is confident of their training and dedication. "We are not among those who shrink back," he says. Who are we among? We are among those who run the race with perseverance (12:1), among "those who have faith and so are saved" (10:39). That constitutes an invitation to name names, to get out the program and identify the players, which is exactly what the Preacher does as he moves to a fresh section of his sermon.

The Great Cloud of Witnesses

HEBREWS 11:1—12:2

There is an old saying among many African American preachers about how to preach a good sermon. The motto has many variations, but it goes something like, "Start low, go slow, reach higher, strike fire, sit down in a storm."

The Preacher of Hebrews is no stranger to this kind of preaching, and he follows this advice in this famous section of the book. This chapter on faith starts low, with the definition of the term "faith," and it goes slow, marching early on to an unhurried cadence of names and events, a rhythmic chronicle of heroes of the faith in days gone by. Then the pace quickens, the pulse races, as the sanctuary is filled with the stories of prophets and saints, the faithful courage of holy ones and martyrs. Finally this passage glows with the white heat of fiery relevance as the Preacher summons the congregation to join the march, to lift high the cross, to run the great race with faith and hope.

Faith (11:1–3)

The Preacher begins by defining faith, the theological quality that will unify this chapter, as "the assurance of things hoped for, the conviction of things not seen." Systematic theologians quite rightly point out that this statement is incomplete. Faith, as a biblical theological concept, is large, round, and complex, and the Preacher's description encompasses but a few degrees of its circumference. But the Preacher is not writing a dogmatics. He is preaching a sermon, and he crafts a working definition of faith that will serve his immediate sermonic goals. Instead of providing a comprehensive definition, the Preacher simply names those aspects of faith he hopes to encourage. He does not need a three-masted doctrinal schooner with all the sails and rigging; he needs a landing craft to get his congregation onto the beachhead that lies on the far horizon.

When the Preacher names faith as the "assurance of things hoped for," he is describing what faith *has*: it already possesses in the present what God has promised for the future. This possession is partly an inward reality and partly an outward force. Inwardly, people of faith have a confidence today, here and now when all hell is breaking loose around us, that the promises of God for peace, justice, mercy, and salvation can be trusted. Faith, in this inward sense, is then a response to the trustworthiness of God. The Preacher is about to give a roll call of the faithful, to name those in every generation who courageously swung out on the vine of God's promises over the chasms of life, trusting that the vine would hold. Time and again, the vine was secure; the promises of God held firm.

But faith as "the assurance of things hoped for" is not just inward confidence, it is also an outward actuality. The word translated "assurance" in this verse, *hypostasis*, was used earlier to describe how the Son is the expression of God's *hypostasis*, God's "very being" (1:3). In other words, faith is the "very being" of God's promises. It is more than the inner confidence that the powers of the world that press down and destroy human life will eventually yield and that God's promises will be fulfilled someday; it is the reality of those promises moving as an advance force and operating behind enemy lines.

Christians, then, have faith as an inward assurance, but they also embody faith as an outward manifestation in the old world of the revolutionary presence of the world to come. Faith as an inward reality sings "We Shall Overcome." Faith as an outward reality marches at

113

Selma. Faith as an inward reality trusts God's promise that "mourning and crying and pain will be no more" (Rev. 21:4). Faith as an outward reality prays boldly for those who mourn, serves tenderly those who weep, works tirelessly to ease the pain of those who are wounded. Inwardly, faith moves hearts; outwardly, faith moves mountains.

If the first part of the Preacher's definition describes what faith *has,* the second phrase describes what faith *perceives.* The affirmation that faith is "the conviction of things not seen" points to faith's capacity to discern realities not visible to the naked eye. "What can be seen," wrote Paul, "is temporary, but what cannot be seen is eternal"; thus, "we walk by faith, not by sight" (2 Cor. 4:18; 5:7). To the eye of faith, the universe is not simply an aimless swirl of energy and matter but a *creation,* an expression of the love of God sustained by God's hidden providence. As the Preacher says, "The worlds were prepared by the word of God, so that what is seen was made from things that are not visible" (11:3), or as Calvin adds, "If God should withdraw His hand a little, all things would immediately perish and dissolve into nothing." To the naked eye, there is trouble all around; "the days of our life," writes the psalmist, "are seventy years, or perhaps eighty, if we are strong; even then their span is only toil and trouble" (Ps. 90:10). To the eye of faith, however, through the toil and trouble another reality can be perceived; in the last words of the priest at the end of Georges Bernanos's *The Diary of a Country Priest,* "Grace is everywhere."

The Preacher knows the difference between what is real and what can be seen. What is real is that Christ is Lord. The heir of all things through whom the world was created now reigns in majesty (1:2–3). But this central reality is hidden from view. As the Preacher said earlier in the sermon, "we do not yet see" the glory of Christ as Lord of all (2:8; also note comments on 2:8b–9). What the naked eye can see, of course, is a world of suffering and setback, violence and hardship. Given the harsh realities of the world, faith is the ability to see with the inner eye, to see what cannot be seen with the natural eye. In Saint-Exupéry's classic story *The Little Prince,* a mysterious fox promises to tell a little boy the greatest of life's secrets. When at long last the secret is told, it is this: "It is only with the heart that one can see rightly; what is essential is invisible to the eye" (Antoine de Saint-Exupéry, *The Little Prince,* p. 70).

Faith, therefore, sings hymns with the theme of "nevertheless": "Though the cause of evil prosper, yet 'tis truth alone is strong; Though her portion be the scaffold, and upon the throne be wrong, Yet that scaffold sways the future, And, behind the dim unknown, Standeth God within the shadow, Keeping watch above his own."

The Preacher is about to start naming names of those in the tradition who exemplified such faith, and he observes about these "ancestors" that it was by faith that they "received approval" (11:2). A more literal translation of this phrase is that these exemplars of faith "received testimony." Who gave this testimony? God did. And in what court? The courtroom of Scripture. God did not swear *on* a Bible; God gave sworn testimony *in* the Bible, bearing witness: "I saw what these people did, and I testify that they were on the true and right path."

Faith's Hall of Heroes (11:4–40)

The Preacher began his sermon, "Long ago God spoke to our ancestors in many and various ways . . ." (1:1). Now the Preacher turns the coin over to show how in many and various ways our ancestors responded to God in faith. With his working definition of faith still ringing in the air (see 11:1–3), he now starts leafing through the Old Testament, stopping here and there to tell the story of one of faith's heroes. Face after face, name after name passes before the congregation–Abel, Noah, Abraham, Isaac, Moses, Rahab–the list goes on. At first it seems that the Preacher is simply moving chronologically through the Bible, picking out names almost at random. But if we stand back from the list, another pattern emerges. The names cluster into four groups of ancestors; each of the first three groups foreshadows one of the faithful virtues that comes to perfection in Jesus. Like Jesus, these forebears in faith were (1) righteous; (2) journeyed obediently in faith; (3) were tested by suffering. The fourth group, a rapid-fire listing of events and names, is a mixture of the three virtues.

1. *Those Who Were Righteous: Abel, Enoch, and Noah* (11:4–7). Jesus, "the apostle and high priest of our confession, was faithful to the one who appointed him" (3:1–2). His obedience showed him to be "faithful over God's house as a Son" (3:6), and he was pleasing to God. The Preacher starts his long list of faithful ancestors with three examples of righteous people who obeyed and thus pleased God:

Abel (11:4). To read the story of Abel in Genesis (4:1–16), one might well wonder why he appears on the Preacher's list of heroes of the faith. Virtually all we know about Abel is that he is the second son of Adam and Eve, was a keeper of sheep, made an acceptable offering from his flock to God, and was murdered by his brother Cain. Abel sings no psalms of faith, gives no testimonies about hope; in fact, as far as Genesis goes, he does not open his mouth at all until after his death. Then his blood cries out from the ground to God, who hears his plea (4:10). If faith is "the assurance of things hoped for, the conviction of

115

things not seen," it is difficult to spot these virtues in the skimpy information we have about Abel.

But the Preacher's mind is working in the other direction. He knows that God accepted Abel's sacrifice and not Cain's. This must mean that God considered Abel to be righteous and approved of him, and since God's approval is one of the marks of faith (11:2), then it follows that Abel was an exemplar of faith.

Having made that case, the Preacher says a curious thing about Abel, that "he died, but through his faith he still speaks." Abel never said a recorded word while alive, but he has evidently become loquacious after death. What does the Preacher mean by the notion that Abel speaks after his death? Does he want to say what countless funeral sermons have said about this text: the good works of a righteous person, in this case Abel's, continue to speak long after the person who performed them is gone? Yes, surely; that is the primary reason Abel's name appears in this list of the faithful. We can admire his faith, learn from it, imitate it; in this way Abel, though dead, still speaks to subsequent generations.

But the Preacher probably also means something more. Without sifting the implications too fine, the Preacher thinks of Abel as more than a memory; he imagines Abel still talking to God. According to the tradition, Abel's blood cried out from the ground to God, calling for justice, appealing to God to set things right and to avenge his murder. The Preacher thinks of this tragic cry for vengeance being voiced by Abel for all human suffering down through the ages.

Abel, then, is an anticipatory shadow of Jesus. Like Jesus, Abel was approved by God and offered a sacrifice that was acceptable to God (indeed, a "better sacrifice," at least than Cain's). Moreover, Abel's blood, like that of Jesus, makes intercession to God. But there the comparison ends. Later in the sermon the Preacher will tell us that Jesus' blood speaks a "better word than the blood of Abel" (12:24). Abel's blood cries out for revenge, but Jesus' blood brings an end to vengeance and grants forgiveness (9:22; 10:10).

Enoch (11:5–6). Genesis 5:24 states, rather mysteriously, that "Enoch walked with God; then he was no more, because God took him." Of the many possible meanings for that verse, the one that gripped the imagination of first-century preachers, including the Preacher of Hebrews, was that Enoch was so pleasing to God ("walked with God" so harmoniously) that he was taken directly to heaven without passing through death's universal door. Viewing the Enoch story this way, the Preacher then employs the same logic he applied to Abel to argue that if Enoch pleased God that much it must have been because of his faith. The Genesis account of Enoch lacks any mention of

116

faith, but that does not bother the Preacher, since "without faith it is impossible to please God" (11:6).

Enoch, then, is another example of a righteous ancestor, one who pleased God, and the Preacher turns this into a lesson for the congregation on how they too can please God. As they approach God, he maintains, they must "believe that he exists and that he rewards those who seek him" (11:6). This kind of language can be misleading, and we must remember that the Preacher is preaching to a struggling congregation, not lecturing before a college debate society. In the Preacher's context, to "believe that God exists and rewards those who seek him" is certainly not an abstract philosophical position on theism, and it means more than saying "yes" when the Gallup pollster asks, "Do you believe in the existence of God?" Rather it means to have confidence in the God who exists, that is, the God who *lives,* and to trust that serving this God really does matter.

In other words, it means having faith, the kind of dynamic faith described at the outset of this passage (11:1). To believe that God exists is to have a profound "conviction of things not seen." To believe that God rewards those who seek him is not to look for crowns or Cadillacs—such baubles and trinkets demean the idea of holy reward—but for a Sabbath rest (see comment on 4:1–11). The reward of faith is the fulfillment of all of God's promises for mercy, peace, and salvation, "the assurance of things hoped for" (see 11:1).

Noah (11:7). The third representative of faithful righteousness is Noah, and what makes him an apt example is his response to the word of God. God told Noah about an event in the unseen world of the future, the coming flood (see Gen. 6:8—9:17). There was no evidence in the visible, sensory world to back up this word, so Noah had a choice to make: to trust what he saw around him with his own eyes or to trust God's word. In short, it was the world or God. Noah chose God and, therefore, did what made no sense whatsoever in worldly terms: he built an ark to weather a storm no one could see coming. In doing so, of course, he in effect "condemned the world" (11:7), rejecting its passing treasure in favor of the eternal promises of God and becoming, as a consequence, "an heir" of heavenly treasure.

But what did Noah inherit? The answer is "the righteousness that is in accordance with faith," which, even for Hebrews, is a tangled phrase. There could be a Pauline flavor here, the idea of righteousness as something God reckons to human beings because of their faith. In other words, the Preacher could be claiming that Noah was justified by faith (see Rom. 3:21–26). It is likelier, though, that the Preacher is closer to the thought of Habakkuk than to that of Paul (see Hab. 2:4),

117

and instead of thinking that Noah was righteous by faith and not by works, he pictures Noah's faith as a power that enabled him to be righteous, to do good works. Noah, through his faith in God's promises, inherited the capacity to live in righteousness, to make the right choices. In sum, Noah, like Abel and Enoch before him, lived by faith, and this was very pleasing to God.

2. *Those Who Journeyed Obediently in Faith: Abraham and Sarah, Isaac and Jacob* (11:8–16). Jesus is "the pioneer and perfector of our faith" (12:2), the one who traveled obediently down through the arc of the great parabola of salvation (see comments on 1:5–14). In the cosmic christology of Hebrews, Jesus left his heavenly home announcing, "I will proclaim your name to my sisters and brothers." He traveled as a stranger and a pilgrim through the wilderness of suffering, but he never wavered, instead fashioning his life into the prayer: "I will put my trust in you." When his journey was complete, he arrived in the great land of his inheritance, the heavenly sanctuary to which he was traveling, carrying with him his sisters and brothers and saying, "Here I am and the children you gave me" (see 2:12–13).

Long before Jesus, but as a foretaste of the good things to come (9:11), Abraham was also a pioneer traveler. He was "called to set out for a place that he was to receive as an inheritance" (11:8). Abraham was being sent on a journey of faith, and we can see here many of the qualities of all faith journeys. First, this journey required a *deep trust* in the One who was sending him. Abraham obeyed, placing his hand in God's hand, even though he did not even know where he was headed (11:8). The journey of faith was also *dislocating*, uprooting his family for generations. He and his son Isaac, and his grandson Jacob, became permanent exiles, never at home, always living in tents, "strangers and foreigners on the earth" (11:13). For survival on the faith journey they were utterly *dependent upon God* for provisions along the way. This was true in the most basic sense, since this was to be a journey taking place over many generations and since Abraham, as well as his wife Sarah, lacked the strength on their own to produce any new generations (11:11–12). Though the path was often mysterious and the travelers sometimes wondered where they would get the energy to go on, this journey's *destination was never in doubt*. This was a forward-looking journey; they gave no thought to what they left behind (11:15), but went in search of a "better country . . . a heavenly one" (11:16), "the city that has foundations, whose architect and builder is God" (11:10).

118

But, alas, they never got there. Abraham and Sarah, Isaac and

Jacob, and all the generations of pilgrims wandering as strangers and exiles "died in faith without having received the promises" (11:13). They could see their destination in the distance; they could almost taste it, but they died along the wayside.

James Michener recounts that medieval pilgrims who traveled the long road from France to the Cathedral of Saint James in Spain would, as they neared the end of their demanding journey, strain their eyes toward the horizon, hoping to see the towers of the long-sought cathedral in the distance. The first one to see would shout, "My joy!" (Michener, *Iberia*, p. 892). In like manner, the Preacher tells us that Abraham and all of his descendants could see the towers of the heavenly city on the far horizon and that they greeted them with shouts of joy (11:13), but they perished without completing the pilgrimage.

This sense of incompletion, the sadness of an unfinished journey, yearns for resolution. Are we simply left with a heartbreaking tale of faithful pilgrims who journeyed in faith but who never arrived at their cherished destination? No, we have a God who keeps promises, a God who sent another pilgrim, the heavenly Son, whose journey of faith led him into the valley of human suffering, into the place where Abraham and all who share his hope were perishing before coming to the end of the road. This pioneer made perfect through suffering (2:10) gathered up Abraham and Sarah, Isaac and Jacob, and all who trust him, and takes them home to the distant city, saying to God, "Here am I and the children you gave me" (2:13).

In Jesus the journey is completed. Jesus became like us "in every respect" (2:17), and he enters into the city of God "not ashamed to call [us] brothers and sisters" (2:11). Abraham and Sarah, Isaac and Jacob looked forward in faith to that city, and "God is not ashamed to be called their God" (11:16).

3. *Those Who Were Tested by Suffering: Abraham, Isaac, Jacob, Joseph, and Moses* (11:17–28). Faith, as the Preacher has said, is a perception that goes beyond sight, a "conviction of things not seen" (11:1). One of the realities that faith views differently is suffering. Seen apart from faith, suffering is always destructive, always leading to no good end. To be sure, some forms of human suffering seem, even to the eyes of faith, to be random, chaotic, and meaningless. But faith sometimes has a different view, seeing suffering as a fire that forges steel or as a tilling of hard ground into the soil of compassion. Because Jesus "himself was tested by what he suffered," the Preacher said earlier in the sermon, he is merciful and "able to help those who are being tested" (2:18).

The Preacher now describes a cluster of faithful ancestors who

119

were tested by suffering, and he begins where he left off in the previous section: with Abraham. This time, however, the Preacher does not tell us of Abraham the pilgrim, but of Abraham who was "put to the test" (11:17). The test in question is, of course, the one recorded in Genesis 22, when God said to Abraham, "Take your son, your only son Isaac, whom you love, and go to the land of Moriah, and offer him there as a burnt offering on one of the mountains that I will show you" (Gen. 22:2).

This difficult Abraham-Isaac story, with its threat of child sacrifice and even the hint of a God who would suggest such a thing, carries a nest of problems for most contemporary readers, but for the Preacher the severe quality of Abraham's testing is, in fact, the point. It is significant to the Preacher that this was a drastic test of Abraham's faith. It was not a minor trial, a little gray cloud on an otherwise brilliant blue sky; it was, rather, a test that ran all the way down to the bottom, that appeared to spell the end of everything—the end of Isaac, the end of God's promise (11:18).

This test was not merely a measure of how tough Abraham was; it brought to the surface the basic framework through which he viewed life. If he brought to this event only a human point of view, then there was but one, inevitable conclusion: this was death, the end, the irreparable unraveling of all his hopes. But Abraham brought another framework: the vision of faith. Faith does not know how or when or where God will fulfill the promise, but faith does not waver from the confidence that God will do it; faith does not let go of "the assurance of things hoped for" (11:1).

In Genesis, Abraham's faith is expressed in his ironic word to Isaac, "God himself will provide the lamb . . . my son" (Gen. 22:8). The Preacher goes even farther and claims that Abraham not only had faith in God's providence, he also glimpsed the possibility of resurrection: "God is able even to raise someone from the dead" (11:19). In other words, because of Abraham's faith the prospect of losing Isaac did not force him to give up or lose his grip on God's promise; it actually refined his faith, teaching him about the possibility of resurrection. In a figurative sense, the Preacher says, Abraham did experience a resurrection, since God gave Isaac back (11:19). This was but a foreshadowing of the real thing, however, the great reversal of history when the God of peace himself did provide the lamb and then "brought back from the dead our Lord Jesus . . ." (12:20).

If by undergoing a test of his faith, Abraham gained a better vision for God's future, that vision was passed along from generation to generation. When the boy Isaac had himself grown old, he faced his own sense of loss. His eyesight was failing and he could no longer see,

120

but his father's faithful vision of God's future remained in him, undimmed. Therefore, "he invoked blessings for the future on Jacob and Esau," his own sons (11:20). When Jacob had grown old, he too faced a loss—a loss of strength of a loss of his own life. He was dying, but the vision of God's future, passed from generation to generation, was not dying. So Jacob, with his own life ebbing away, reverently bowed "over the top of his staff" and blessed his grandsons, the sons of Joseph (11:21; see Gen. 48:8–22). As for Joseph, when he faced, down in Egypt, his own loss, his own approaching death, he did not view this as the end of everything, but looked out toward the horizon of God's future with the eyes of faith. Staring into the grave, he saw grace. If his great-grandfather's test had provided a glimpse of the resurrection, Joseph's own impending death gave him a glimpse of the promised land; he "made mention of the exodus of the Israelites" and ordered that, when that time arrived, his bones were to be carried into the land of promise (11:22).

For an additional example of faith under pressure, the Preacher turns to Moses and his family. Moses plays a key role, of course, in the story of faith, but that role was profoundly threatened from the moment of his birth because of the standing order of the Egyptian king to kill all male Hebrew infants (Ex. 1:8–22).

When Moses was born, though, his parents hid him for three months (11:23; the Preacher here uses the Septuagint, which attributes this hiding to both parents, unlike the Hebrew text, which mentions only Moses' mother). Why did they hide him? The Preacher gives two reasons, one biblical and one not. According to Exodus, the hiding took place because Moses was "a fine baby," or "beautiful" as the Preacher puts it, and thus the infant Moses was all the more valuable and all the more vulnerable. To this motivation the Preacher adds that Moses' parents "were not afraid of the king's edict" (11:23). He probably borrowed that virtue from the previous account of the two fearless midwives, Shiphrah and Puah (Ex. 1:15–22), but the theological point remains regardless of the Preacher's source: Moses' parents exercised faith under fire, acted boldly on behalf of God's future rather than knuckling under to the evil powers of the world.

Their son learned that lesson well. When Moses became an adult, he too bucked the powers-that-be at every turn. The Preacher cites three examples:

First, given the choice between being a privileged son of the Egyptian royal family or being a child of the suffering family of God, he chose his true identity, his family of birth. There are two theological insights to be gained from this decision of Moses. One, the

121

Preacher's congregation is facing the same choice. Do they stay in the family of God, where day in and day out there is suffering and testing, where constantly they are exposed to a wearying struggle against discouragement and sin (see 12:3–4), or do they walk out the church door into what appears to be an easier, less fatiguing style of life? The Preacher's assessment of Moses' choice is actually his verdict on the congregation's option: Moses faithfully and wisely chose "rather to share ill-treatment with the people of God than to enjoy the fleeting pleasures of sin" (11:25).

A further theological insight is that Moses here provides a kind of reverse image of Christ. Moses, who was born as the child of slaves, chose a life of suffering with his people rather than the temporary, transient, "fleeting pleasures" of life in the royal palace. Moses actually suffered this abuse, claims the Preacher, in anticipation of the Christ, "for he was looking ahead to the reward" (11:26). And when the Christ came, Moses and all others with faith received that reward. Jesus, who was born a royal son, chose "for a little while" to be a slave, under the rule of suffering and death, in order that all human beings under the slavery of sin might be set free and enter with confidence into the heavenly palace, no longer as slaves but as heirs of the promises and children of the heavenly King.

Second, Moses also "left Egypt, unafraid of the king's anger" (11:27). The problem is, the biblical story of Moses' departure from Egypt after he killed an Egyptian overseer explicitly indicates that Moses was, in fact, afraid (Ex. 2:11–15). Either the Preacher is "so impressed by Moses' general courage and faith" that he overlooks the details of the text (as Ellingworth thinks) or he is drawing upon extrabiblical traditions and stories about Moses that play down Moses' fear (as Attridge suggests). What really matters is not the Preacher's source but his theological point: because he was faithful, because "he saw him who was invisible" (11:27), Moses was not fearful.

Under the pressure of testing and suffering, the naked eye can see only the oppressor. We can see only the jackboot of tyranny, or the scars of child abuse, or the x-rays with the spot on the lung. Faith sees all that; it does not pretend there is no Pharaoh, no evil, no disease. But faith also sees God, the God who promises to bring an end to all that harms and destroys, the God who provided a great high priest "who in every respect has been tested as we are" and who enables us to "receive mercy and find grace to help in time of need" (4:15–16). Like Moses, the faithful in all times and places perceive "him who is invisible" and have the "conviction of things not seen" (11:1, 27).

122

Third, finally, Moses "by faith . . . kept the Passover and the sprinkling of blood" (11:28). The Passover was, of course, the ritual commemorating the sparing of the Hebrews when God destroyed the first-born of all the households and flocks of Egypt (Ex. 12:1–28). Two main theological factors are at work here. First, in the midst of suffering and death, Moses again has his eye of faith fixed on a different reality; the Passover, as a symbol of salvation, is the sign of that faithful vision.

The Preacher also has the underlying conviction that it is a dangerous thing for sinful humanity, apart from the perfection made possible through Christ (10:14), to approach or to come into contact with the holiness of God. In the next chapter, in fact, the Preacher will contrast the free access Christians have to God with the old covenant perils of "touching the holy" (12:20). Through faith, we "have confidence to enter the sanctuary" (10:19); apart from faith, God's holy touch burns as "a consuming fire" (12:29), and "it is a fearful thing to fall into the hands of the living God" (10:31). Through faith, God's holy testing brings strength; apart from faith, God's testing destroys. Moses observed the Passover to insure that "the destroyer of the firstborn would not touch the firstborn of Israel" (11:28). As such, he pointed toward the new Passover. If in the first Passover the blood of the lamb kept God from touching the flesh of the faithful, in the new Passover God through the Son became human flesh so that we might not fear his touch, so that we may not dread destruction but "may receive mercy and find grace in time of need" (4:16).

4. *A Host of Witnesses* (11:29–38). In terms of the African American preachers' saying, the Preacher of Hebrews has "started low" with a definition of faith (11:1–3). Then he proceeded to "go slow" by recounting in some detail the stories of Abel, Enoch, Noah, the patriarchs, and Moses (11:4–28). Now it is time to quicken the pace, to "reach higher," and a reading of even the English translation of this next section will disclose that the Preacher is doing just that. Instead of stories, we now get phrases; instead of more languid narration, we get the sharp staccato beat of crisp declarations. The Preacher begins to preach his sermon with a rhythm line similar to the one Vachel Lindsay used in his poetry:

> Oh, shout Salvation! it was good to see
> Kings and Princes by the Lamb set free.
> The banjos rattled and the tambourines
> Jing-jing-jangled in the hands of Queens.
> (Lindsay, p. 504)

The Preacher knows that he is bringing his congregation into the dialogue, lifting them into ecstasy; that is what he is after. Even in the written version, there are the unmistakable signs of the Preacher's calls followed by implied responses:

123

CALL: "And what more should I say?" (11:32)

RESPONSE: "Tell it all, brother, tell it all!"

CALL: "O brothers and sisters, time would fail me to tell it all . . ." (11:32)

RESPONSE: "No, brother, tell it all!"

CALL: "I'd have to tell about Gideon and Barak, Samson, Jepthah, of David and Samuel and the prophets—" (11:32)

RESPONSE: "Yes! Tell it all, brother. Preach on!"

CALL: "I'd have to tell about those whose faith conquered kingdoms and shut up lion's mouths. I'd have to tell about women who were tortured, men who were mighty in war, children of God who were flogged and stoned. . . . O, I tell you brothers and sisters, the world was not worthy of them, not worthy at all!" (11:33–38)

RESPONSE: "No, no, not at all!"

The names and events in this fourth section of the passage blend the three virtues of faith developed in the first sections:

a. *Those Who Were Righteous.* The Israelites were, like Abel, approved by God because of their faith, and therefore they "passed through the Red Sea as if it were dry land." The Egyptians, like Cain, were not approved by God, and "they were drowned." The righteous encircled Jericho, and the city fell. Rahab, a prostitute and a Gentile, an outsider in every way, was an insider through faith, and obediently received the Hebrew spies. Therefore, she "did not perish with those who were disobedient." In addition, by faith the righteous "conquered kingdoms, administered justice, and obtained promises."

b. *Those Who Journeyed Obediently.* By faith "the people passed through the Red Sea" on the way to the land of promise. By faith, they "went about in skins of sheep and goats." Like the patriarchs who "were strangers and foreigners on the earth," they "wandered in deserts and mountains."

c. *Those Who Were Tested by Suffering.* The Preacher tells of those who had their faith tested and purified by suffering, people who "quenched raging fire, escaped the edge of the sword, won strength out of weakness, and became mighty in war." He speaks of women who had faith like Abraham, who in the time of his own testing "considered the fact that God is able even to raise someone from the dead" (11:19). These women "received their dead by resurrection" (referring no doubt to the widow of Zarephath in 1 Kings 17:17–24 and the

124

Shunammite woman in 2 Kings 4:8–37). He mentions others who were "tortured, refusing to accept release" because they were waiting for a "better resurrection" than the momentary, transient pleasure of freedom. He evokes the memory of still others who "suffered mocking and flogging, and even chains and imprisonment," who were "stoned to death . . . sawn in two" and were "destitute, persecuted, tormented."

The Congregation
Joins the Chain (11:39—12:2)

In his poem "Our Children, Coming of Age," Wendell Berry begins:

> In the great circle, dancing in
> and out of time, you move now
> toward your partners, answering
> the music suddenly audible to you
> that only carried you before
> and will carry you again.
> (Berry, p. 264)

In a rousing section of the sermon, the Preacher has been drumming the beat of the pilgrims of old. Marching forward through the Old Testament, the Preacher has mustered the faithful—Abel, Enoch, and Noah, Abraham and Sarah, Moses and the prophets. The Preacher's pace has quickened as the list of the righteous draws closer and closer to the present.

But just as this parade of faith has nearly reached the church door, the drumbeat stops and the Preacher halts—or, more accurately, *pauses*. He stares at the congregation for half a beat, then sweeps his arm in a slow backward movement, as if to wend his way back down the pathway his words have just traveled, as if to gather in a single gesture the whole assembly of faithful ancestors lined up as far as the eye can see, as if to retrace in "the great circle, dancing in and out of time" the arc he has just traversed of all the men and women of old who trusted in the promises of God. Then he says, slowly and deliberately, these telling words: "Yet all these, though they were commended for their faith, did not receive what was promised" (11:39).

All that faith, all that righteousness, all that suffering, all those endless miles of journeying, and they "did not receive what was promised."

The congregation has heard this before, specifically about the patriarchs (11:13), but even so, the protest "But why?" begins to rise in
their throats. Before it can find a voice, though, the Preacher explains: "God provided something better . . ." (11:40). The congregation knows, of course, that the Preacher means Jesus. The word "better" connected to Jesus has been a constant refrain: Jesus is "better
than the angels" (1:4), and he introduces a "better hope" (7:19) and
guarantees a "better covenant" (7:22) with "better promises" (8:6)
and sealed with "better sacrifices" (9:23), and all of this allows us to
possess an inheritance from God that is "better " (10:34). So it comes
as no surprise that these faithful ancestors did not receive the
promise until the coming of Jesus. As people of faith, they were leaning forward in hope, searching for no earthly homeland but for the
city whose architect and builder is God (11:10), waiting for a "better
resurrection." Their hopes could not be fulfilled; their quest could
not be satisfied; their desire for resurrection could not be met until
there was a better high priest, "a Son who has been made perfect forever" (7:28).

But if the congregation was not surprised by the Preacher's affirmation that God had provided "something better," namely Jesus,
they were probably astounded by his next statement: "so that they
would not, apart from us, be made perfect" (11:40). The congregation could surely see how we need *them*. These biblical ancestors are,
after all, the heroes and representatives of faith; we live by their example. The congregation could also stretch their minds to understand how even these faithful people of old needed *Jesus*. They were
worshiping in temporary tents with repeated sacrifices, leaning in
hope toward the better and lasting sacrifice that Jesus made, the sacrifice of himself that at long last redeemed the whole gathering of the
faithful "from the transgressions under the first covenant" (9:15).
What was staggering to the imagination was the claim that these
faithful of old somehow need *us*, that "apart from us" they cannot be
made perfect.

The Preacher is not implying, of course, that we redeem Abraham
and Moses; only Christ sanctifies and saves. What he is saying is that
the high-priestly ministry of Jesus Christ establishes a great unbroken
cord of faith that stretches from the beginning of human history all the
way into the heavenly sanctuary in the City of God, where the cord has
been securely fastened and anchored by Jesus (6:19–20). The
"parabola of salvation," which has provided the underlying structure
for so much of this sermon (see comments on 1:5–14), now turns out
to be not just the pathway traveled by the Son, not just something

126

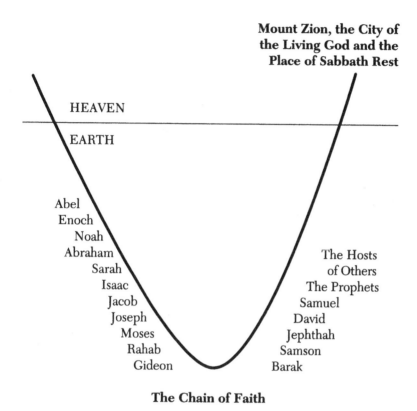

Mount Zion, the City of the Living God and the Place of Sabbath Rest

HEAVEN

EARTH

Abel
Enoch
Noah
Abraham
Sarah
Isaac
Jacob
Joseph
Moses
Rahab
Gideon

The Hosts
of Others
The Prophets
Samuel
David
Jephthah
Samson
Barak

The Chain of Faith

Figure 6

Jesus forms, but a chain of faithful people holding onto the cord and to each other:

Abel, a man of faith, took his place on the great "parabola" grasping the cord of salvation with both hands. Then Enoch stepped forward, and overlapping one hand on that of Abel, he too took his spot on the chain. And so Noah, Abraham and Sarah, Moses and all the rest assumed their places on the cord. The links are formed by faithful people, hand in hand, generation after generation, holding fast to each other and to "our confession" (4:14). It is by this cord of faith that Jesus brings "many children to glory" (2:10) and makes all of the saints perfect (10:14). There is a gap in the line of the faithful, a space in the arc to be filled by those who hear the gospel. We

127

are to step up to the cord and join with those who through the ages held on by faith. It is in this sense of forming the unbroken community of faith that our ancestors "would not, apart from us, be made perfect."

So now this great cord is passing through the sanctuary of the Preacher's congregation, and it is their turn to form the human links of faith that join the whole chain to "Jesus the pioneer and perfecter of our faith." As Wendell Berry put it, "You move now toward your partners, answering the music suddenly audible to you."

The time has come, then, for the Preacher to "strike fire," to stir the souls of his congregation, to get them up out of the pews and on the march to Zion. He does so by subtly shifting the metaphor. Instead of the image of a pilgrimage or of an unbroken chain of faith, the Preacher now takes his congregation to the sports arena (as he did earlier; see comment on 10:36) and drafts them as the final runners in a great relay race of faith. The baton has been passed from Abel to Enoch to Noah to Abraham, each runner handing it on to the next. Now it is the congregation's turn to run. The previous runners have taken their seats in the stadium—"we are surrounded by so great a cloud of witnesses"—and all are watching to see how we will perform.

The Preacher knows that it is late in the day, and that we have already run several sprints and dashes. We are winded and tired, but this is the race that counts, so we are to strip off anything that would slow us down—all the weighty encumbrances and shackling sins (12:1)—and run our portion of the race with endurance.

The trail has already been blazed; the path of the race has already been forged by Jesus. He is the lead runner, and he shows us where to go, since he is the "pioneer," the one who sets the course. He also shows us how to run, since he is the one who runs the race with flawless form, the "perfecter of our faith." Indeed, it is Christ who makes it possible for us to run at all.

Moreover, he teaches us how to handle the long hills, how to get a second wind when the going gets hard: keep your eyes on the prize, never lose sight of the Sabbath rest that awaits those who endure (see comments on 4:1–11). Jesus himself kept his eyes on the prize, "the joy that was set before him." The goal of the race for Jesus was not only a seat "at the right hand of the throne of God" (1:3; 12:2), but the joy of bringing with him the other runners, of "bringing many children to glory" (2:10), of crossing the finish line and saying, "Here am I and the children God has given me" (2:13).

For the sake of this joy, then, he endured the disgrace and pain

128

of the cross, "disregarding its shame" (12:2). The shame of the cross was a twofold shame. First, the cross was a cruel instrument of capital punishment. Jesus did not die of natural causes or in a boating accident; he was executed as a criminal, as a menace to human society. It was, by worldly standards, the kind of death definitive of shame.

Second, shame is an experience, a human emotion, connected to public exposure. When the judging eyes of others turn our way, when people wag their heads at us, saying, "What has happened to you? We always thought more of you than this," when we are "caught out in the open" without the shield of our respectability, naked and unprotected, we feel embarrassed and ashamed. When Jesus hung on the cross, he was exposed to the pitying, judging, reviling gaze of others. Passersby wagged their heads and mocked him. Religious leaders derided him and laughed at his weakness. Common criminals taunted him. It is a common custom to place a hood over the head of one being executed so that he will at least be able to preserve some small hold on human dignity, at least be able to avoid meeting the shame-filled gaze of the executioner. But Jesus was given no hood, allowed no relief from the public humiliation.

But Jesus disregarded the shame for the sake of the joy set before him. Human beings stood at the foot of the cross and shamed him, but for the sake of saving humanity he endured the shame. Sin coiled around the human heart and struck at Jesus, but he disregarded the shame so that he might provide an atonement for sin. People loyal to the government and to religion schemed to put Jesus to a shameful death, but he disregarded the shame so that he might rule with mercy as Lord of all and open the door of welcome in the true sanctuary.

When we see the disciplined, loving, strong, merciful, and faithful way that Jesus ran the race, we are motivated to lace up our running shoes, to grasp the baton, and to sprint for the finish line. The only thing that would cause us to "shrink back" is our old problem of weariness. The race is hard, our muscles are tired, and we lose heart. If the race of faith is so joyful, we wonder, why does it have to be so hard? And that is the question to which the Preacher turns next.

In the Training Room

HEBREWS 12:3–17

According to the old tale, on the wall of a city telephone booth was plastered a sticker that read, "If you are tired of sin, read John 3:16." Below this was scribbled a handwritten note: "If you are *not* tired of sin, call 555-1176."

The Preacher's congregation is tired all right, but they are not exactly tired of sin and it is not precisely accurate to say that they are tired of sainthood either. What they are tired of is the *struggle* between the two, the constant warfare that trying to be faithful entails. We do not know the specific nature of the battles they were fighting, but as we noted earlier, this young Christian community was paying some kind of price for their faith that was increasingly taking its toll on their hope and endurance (see comments on 10:26–39).

Why doesn't the Preacher explicitly describe their struggles and sufferings? Maybe he does not have to; after all, his congregation already knows them full well. But his reticence may also be due to the fact that the Preacher thinks of these local conflicts as the manifestation of a more general "struggle against sin" (12:4). He has already alluded to the fact that they are "partners" in persecution with others (10:33), and there is a sense in which, whatever the nature of their particular trouble, they are joined in suffering with Christians in all times and places.

True participation in the Christian faith always carries a price. When the experience of Christians in many cultures and settings is surveyed, the currency changes but the fact of costly commitment remains. Sometimes the cost is *financial*. There are jobs Christians will not do, deals they will not make, promotions they will not get, conspiracies they will not join. Sometimes the cost is *social*. Families have been known to disown converts, people of one religion often avoid adherents of another, and, as one wry commentator observed, "In urbane societies at parties, one can talk about any topic one desires, no matter how much of a taboo it may be. If, however, you mention God more than twice, you probably won't be invited back."

In other cultural settings, the cost can be *intellectual and emo-*

130

tional. It is far more demanding, mentally and affectively, to figure out how to love one's enemies than the relatively easier task of devising ways to get even. Also, true prayer can be exhausting and has often been described as an almost muscular struggle, with images drawn from the world of wrestling or even warfare. What is more, in any given situation, the cross is the heaviest piece of furniture to move, and Christians are charged with the considerable task of picking it up and carrying it every single day. The cost can also be *political.* There are appointments for which Christians will not appear on the short list. There are powers they will not exercise, lords they will not serve, even for a moment.

So Christian commitment carries a price tag, but, of course, Christians are not always willing to pay the cost. The price can seem too high or, like a commuter on a toll road, one can finally grow weary of paying it every day. Most of the time, though, what erodes confidence is the loss of hope. It begins to seem futile to pay the cost when nothing changes, when the problems seem unfixable and the powers-that-be are too strong; it feels like pouring hard-earned assets down a bottomless pit. "If you're going to live for God in the twentieth century," David Buttrick said in a sermon, "you're in for a fight. . . . A Bible study circle up against the corporate wealth of Wall Street; a sweet sermon on sacrifice versus a million dollar advertising campaign bought and paid for by Mobil Oil Company. . . . Good heavens, by all odds, we haven't got a chance!" (Buttrick, "Up Against the Powers That Be," pp. 220–21).

So for all these reasons and more, Christians grow weary and lose heart. They get tired of the struggle, tired of fighting the problems in the city, tired of serving the needs of people who turn away without a word of thanks, tired of battling to keep the church school going, tired of making visits to people who are "shopping for a church," tired of battling their own addictions, their own cravings, tired of fighting off their own desire just to put down the plow and rest along the way. Why not let somebody else break up this rocky ground?

For the most part, weary Christians are not going to do anything dramatic; they are not planning to join a witches' coven or write a tract on the satisfactions of atheism or establish a new and less demanding religion. They are not going to go away mad; they are just going to go away. The Preacher is not concerned about the few who make a scene and slam the front door of the church on the way out; they were never really with us in the first place. He is concerned, however, about those who slip quietly out the side door, never to return. He is concerned about those who pour their lives into the offering plate but never receive the blessing, those who have all the scars but none of the hope.

131

The Preacher's congregation, after getting up morning after morning and finding that the world of resistance and suffering has not gone away during the night, greets each new dawn not with energy anymore but with drooping hands and weak knees.

Why Is the Christian Life So Hard? (12:3–11)

In response to his congregation's fatigue, to their wearied bewilderment over the hardships of the Christian life, the Preacher does two things:

First, he once again asks the congregation to remember the example of Jesus. In the footrace image that dominated the previous passage, Jesus was viewed as the lead runner, and there too the congregation was invited to draw inspiration from the endurance of Jesus (see 12:2). Here, though, the metaphor is not racing but battle, but once again the disciple is invited to imitate the master. In effect the Preacher says, "I know that you are meeting resistance and getting shot at from all sides, but just remember how much enemy fire Jesus drew on his way to victory, and take heart" (12:3). In fact, whatever hostility the congregation is encountering, it has not yet resulted in bloodshed (12:4); the hostility encountered by Jesus, of course, did (9:14, 22).

Samuel Shoemaker was once asked why he poured his life and ministry into the wretched of New York City. Shoemaker's health was failing and his sense of the city's need overwhelming and discouraging. "Why don't you just run away from it all before you are broken by this inhuman burden you have placed on yourself?" a friend wondered. "I would like to run away from it all," Shoemaker is said to have replied, "but a strange man on the cross won't let me" (Sweet, *Strong in the Broken Places*, p. 15).

Second, the Preacher provides a framework of meaning for their suffering. All suffering is painful to the body and a challenge to the spirit, but the suffering that tears away at the soul is the suffering that has no purpose. People can endure intense distress and pain if they know it is not meaningless.

When a hospital patient recovering from surgery rings the call bell and asks the nurse why the pain is so bad, the most reassuring truth the nurse can provide is to say that the pain is a sure sign that healing is taking place. The Preacher here is a night nurse coming to the bedside of his hurting congregation to reassure them that the pain they feel is not a destructive anguish but a healing one. Or to use the image in the text itself, the Preacher is like the wise next-door neighbor of young children who are complaining to him that their parents are too hard on them, too quick to punish, too ready to give them difficult chores, reassuring them that their parents' discipline springs from love and concern.

Indeed, the heart of the Preacher's encouragement comes from Proverbs 3:11–12 (quoted in 12:5–6), which is a word about the parental discipline of God, a word that the Preacher says the congregation has somehow forgotten in all of its frazzled complaining about suffering (12:5). The sum total of the quotation and the Preacher's comments on it (12:7–11) is that much of the suffering they are experiencing may seem like it is generated at random from the opposition forces in the world, but it is actually the expression of God's parental discipline, which is a good thing.

Why should we think of God's strict rod of correction as a good thing? The Preacher ticks off three reasons. First, it is a sure sign that we are truly God's children. The only children who are undisciplined are those who are unloved and abandoned (12:8). Second, we can recognize God's pattern from our own family upbringing. As children we were rarely enthusiastic about parental control and correction, but looking back on it we recognize that it was in our own best interests (12:9–10). And third, the end result of God's discipline is worth the pain. The harvest of God's punishment is that we "share his holiness" (12:10) and taste the "peaceful fruit of righteousness" (12:11).

The phrases "share God's holiness" and "the peaceful fruit of righteousness" are theological expressions that carry some heft, but here it is probably best not to overinterpret them but to understand them in a more homey way. This is a practical section of the sermon, and the down-to-earth question before the house is: Why do good parents (including God) discipline their children? The answer is that good parents exercise discipline because they want their children to grow up to be like them, to share their values, commitments, and way of life. Nothing honors a schoolteacher more than if one of his children chooses to follow in his footsteps and make teaching her life. Nothing touches a mother with love of gardening like seeing her young son in the backyard digging in the soil "just like my mom."

As a parent, God is the same way. We are disciplined so that we will grow up to be like God, to love what God loves, to mature into the "image of God," to "share in God's holiness." God, of course, gardens the whole cosmos: plowing, planting seeds, and watering in all the worlds that are. We have only a tiny plot of land and a little spade, but we can still work our small parcel in the same caring way that God works the great fields. God's discipline, says the Preacher, is correcting our mistakes and teaching us how to till the soil.

133

Also, good parents discipline their children because they want them to grow up to have a life of meaning and joy; they want them to come to a place that is deeply satisfying and filled with good things. Wise parents know that what looks attractive to a child may not be good in the long run, and, conversely, what looks unappealing to a child may be just what the child needs. So rules and demands, words of advice and acts of discipline are not arbitrary but, rather, are like guidewires on a sapling, designed to help the young tree grow strong and true.

Again, so it is with God. God wants us to have "the peaceful fruit of righteousness," which means that God desires for us a good life of virtue and value, one that provides a sense of purpose and a peaceful confidence of a life well spent.

We need to remind ourselves that the Preacher is addressing a pastoral problem, not writing a theodicy. Taken as an absolute principle, the idea that all human suffering is actually the hand of a loving God teaching us good lessons is untenable. It is difficult, for example, to see the useful lessons in the gas chambers of a death camp or in infant melanoma. But the Preacher is not trying to account for all suffering; the Preacher is trying to make sense of his congregation's struggle to be faithful and not to fall away from the faith. What he says about painful experiences is not true of all suffering, but it is true of some. Indeed, more times than we are sometimes ready to acknowledge, we look back on a season of sorrow and realize that because of it something good and strong and true has been formed in us. The Preacher wants us to know that our best response to that is not, "Sorrow has its lessons," but "Praise be to our loving God."

Limping toward
the Finish Line (12:12–17)

At the beginning of this chapter, the Preacher roused his congregation with the exciting picture of a footrace. Banners were flying, the stadium was filled with spectators, and the members of the congregation were urged to respond like trained athletes: stripping off the weights and running like greyhounds toward the tape (12:1). But now, after wrestling once more with the vexing problem of suffering and pain (12:3–11), the Preacher advances a somewhat different image: the Christian as a runner with a limp.

In many major cities there are annual marathons involving thousands of runners. At the head of the pack are the world class marathoners. Lean and speedy, they race through the course with astonishing swiftness. At the rear of the throng, however, the picture is quite different. There we find the ordinary runners, a few more years under the belt perhaps, a little extra weight over the belt, a lot more pausing to sip water and to catch one's breath. There are also the contestants on crutches and in wheelchairs, courageously out on the course nonetheless. Sometimes one of the runners near the back will grow weak from the heat or faint from exhaustion. When this happens, other runners will stop to help out, compassion being more important than competition in the rear of the marathon.

The Preacher now wants his congregation to know that the great race of the Christian life is often more like the back of the marathon than like the front. By the power of Christ, weary, discouraged, and somewhat out-of-shape Christians are encouraged nevertheless to "lift your drooping hands and strengthen your weak knees" (12:12, using language drawn from Isa. 35:3). God's race is not the Olympics; it is the Special Olympics, and runners who are "lame," that is, encumbered in so many ways, are encouraged to get out on the track and to "make straight paths for your feet" (12:13, with the image taken from Prov. 4:26).

If anybody in the congregation is of a mind to say, "I'm too weak to race. I have a bad leg. Get somebody else," the Preacher responds, "Pick up your bed and run." In the Christian faith, if you play hurt, you end up healed; if you stay on the sidelines, the injury just gets worse (12:13).

What does running the race with a limp look like in actual practice? How does one, running there at the back of the pack, "make straight paths for your feet" when one of your feet is a bit askew? The Preacher states that running the Christian race means, in essence, paying graceful attention to the other runners around you. We are to try to make peace to the best of our ability with everyone in the community and act toward others in the everyday relationships of life in the holy ways of mercy and justice that we have seen in Jesus (12:14). Occasions will open up that are opportunities for compassion and faithful encouragement to others, windows of grace, and we are not to let any of them pass by; we are to "see to it that no one fails to obtain the grace of God" (12:15). When the potential for bitterness and rancor that lies beneath the surface of every human community begins to sprout poison ivy, we are not to fertilize and water it (12:16; see Deut. 29:17).

At this point we can almost hear the wheels whirring in the Preacher's head. His earlier picture of Christians as people running with a limp (12:13) calls to his mind old Jacob, walking into the dawn after a night of God-wrestling, "limping because of his hip" but with a divine blessing (Gen. 32:22–32). And the thought of Jacob leads the Preacher to think of his twin, Esau, who received a quick notation in

135

the previous chapter's roll call of the faithful, but who was promptly dropped (see 11:20). Now we are about to learn why.

The congregation is to be careful not to become like Esau. In the Old Testament, Esau is bathed in an unfavorable light, but that is nothing compared to what happens to him in later tradition. He became a symbol for just about everything that can go wrong with a human being; as the Preacher says, he was "immoral and godless." The main reason the Preacher brings him up, however, is because of Esau's shortsighted action of selling "his birthright for a single meal" (12:16; see Gen. 25:29–34). In other words, when they were handing out T-shirts for the big marathon, Esau was in the chow line and missed the race. When they were passing out blessings, Esau was too tired and hungry to pay attention, and he lost his inheritance. This is, of course, what the Preacher fears his congregation is about to do. Like Esau, they are feeling some immediate pressures, some hunger pangs, and the temptation is foolishly and shortsightedly to abandon the faith for something more immediately gratifying.

If they do, if they limp off the track and head for the pub, they will miss what waits for them at the finish line, "the joy set before us" (12:2). To make sure they know what they will be missing, the Preacher now warms up the slide projector to give them, in the next section of the sermon, a glimpse of the sights ahead, a preview of coming attractions.

The Two Mountains

HEBREWS 12:18–29

Robert Frost's memorable "The Road Not Taken" begins, "Two roads diverged in a yellow wood." The Preacher's congregation is not in a yellow wood—they are in a heat-baked and exhausting spiritual desert—but they have come to a place where two roads diverge, and like the traveler in Frost's poem, the one they choose to take will make "all the difference."

The signpost that points down one fork reads "To Mount Sinai," and the sign pointing down the other fork reads "To Mount Zion." As the advertisements for some fancy computer software once asked, "Where to you want to go today?" Mount Sinai and Mount Zion are metaphors for the old and the new covenants (see 8:1—10:39), and the

Preacher has been laboring throughout the whole sermon to get us to go to Mount Zion. He is fearful, though, that we will choose the other path. The road to Mount Sinai is well-traveled, downhill most of the way, has plenty of fast food restaurants, and looks a great deal more comfortable than the rocky and narrow high road that climbs up to Mount Zion.

A Field Trip to Zion (12:18–24)

In order to urge his congregation to choose the high road, to travel to Mount Zion, the Preacher uses a classic travel agent's strategy: get them to imagine that they are already there. Think of a video travelogue that opens with the scene of a harried man driving in rush hour traffic. Suddenly the scene dissolves to a shot of a lovely lagoon, a picture-perfect sailboat bobbing gently at anchor. A narrator's voice is saying, "Forget the traffic and the tension, forget the phones and the faxes. You aren't at the office any more; you have come to the magical island of St. Lucia." The fact is you *aren't* on the magical island of St. Lucia; you are in your den watching this on TV. But in your imagination you are already taking a dip in the warm Caribbean waters, and this whets your appetite all the more to go.

So the Preacher begins his travelogue with a word even more dramatic than, "You aren't at the office any more." He begins, "You have not come to something that can be touched, a blazing fire, and darkness, and gloom, and a tempest. . . . You have come to Mount Zion and to the city of the living God . . ." (12:18, 22). In the Old Testament, Sinai is, of course, a good thing—the place of the giving of the law. But the Preacher employs Sinai as a negative sign, a symbol of everything that goes awry in religion when it is severed from the high-priestly ministry of Christ (7:1—10:39).

What is wrong with Sinai? It is a place of fear. Human beings come to Sinai as perpetually unclean sinners, and therefore the holiness of God at Sinai is a holy terror. To touch Sinai is fatal, and any animal that ventures out onto this holy ground is destroyed (see Exod. 19:12–13). Sinai is filled with sights and sounds that inject horror into the heart. Even though a fire blazes there, it is still a place of gloom and darkness (12:18; see Deut. 4:11–12; 5:22–23). Streaks of jagged lightning split the sky, thunder rumbles, and a trumpet blows so loudly it scares the wits out of people (12:19; see Exod. 19:16), but the trumpet and the storm are mild compared to the stark terror of God's voice (12:19). In Exodus, the people beg Moses not to let God speak directly to them

137

because, as they say, "We will die" (12:19). Even Moses shook with fear on Sinai (12:21; see Deut. 9:19).

But the good news, says the Preacher, is that we are *not* at Sinai; we have come to Mount Zion. The word translated "come" is not lightly chosen. It is best translated "approach" and it is one of the Preacher's favorite words to refer to the bold and confident access to God possible in Christ: "Let us therefore approach the throne of grace with boldness" (4:16); "[Christ] is able for all time to save those who approach God through him" (7:25); "let us approach [the house of God] with a true heart in full assurance of faith" (10:22).

When we approach Mount Zion, what do we find? The Preacher describes this destination using four pairs of terms:

1. *The Mountain and the City* (12:22a). The time of King David's reign was remembered as Israel's Camelot. Jerusalem and Mount Zion were more than places then, they were symbols of ideals in government and worship, prosperity and peace. But now, under the new covenant, they refer to more than the reign of David and the earthly city; they speak of the rule of God and the heavenly Jerusalem. No one cries out in fear on Zion's hill, as they did at Sinai, terrified that God's word and presence bring death; this is the city of the *living* God.

2. *The Angels and the Firstborn* (12:22b–23a). The citizens of this heavenly city are the angels, not just a few of them but thousands upon thousands, and not the dour and pious messengers of countless paintings and movies but frolicking, laughing, festive angels. None of the gloom of old Sinai can be found here. Along with angels are gathered "the assembly of the firstborn who are enrolled in heaven." This is the Preacher's way of talking about Christians who have gone to their reward, the baptized saints of God who, through baptism, belong to Jesus Christ, the true "firstborn" (see 1:6), who are "enrolled" in the Book of Life.

Some who have described Christian worship have drawn a similar picture to the Preacher's view of Zion. In heaven right now, they say, there is a festive and ceaseless party underway, with angels fluttering around in joy and the saints swinging from the chandeliers. Every so often the floor of heaven opens up and this whole spree descends into ordinary time and space; this is Christian worship.

3. *The Judge and the Acquitted* (12:23b). In the courts of Zion there is but one verdict: not guilty. Those who have come to this city have passed through the gateway of the great high priest, Jesus, who has "perfected for all time those who are sanctified" (10:14). Down at Sinai, the laws are tough and the judgments are harsh. No human being can stand under them, and everyone has to do some time. But here in Zion, the God who sent the Son is the judge, and the Son, who was

138

"for a little while was made lower than the angels" (2:9), has already done the time on our behalf.

4. *Jesus and the Sprinkled Blood* (12:24). There is blood on Sinai, and there is blood on Mount Zion, but it isn't the same blood. On Sinai there is the blood of violence, tragedy, and perpetual sin. There is Abel's blood that cries out for revenge. There is the endless flow of the blood sacrifices that "cannot perfect the conscience of the worshiper" (9:9). On Mount Zion, by contrast, there is the "sprinkled blood" of Jesus (see 9:11–14) offered "once for all" (10:10), blood that purifies the "conscience from dead works to worship the living God" (9:14). By his blood, Jesus has become the mediator of a new covenant (see 9:15–22), a covenant of forgiveness, a covenant in which "those who are called . . . receive the promised eternal inheritance" (9:15).

There is worship every day, all day, in the true sanctuary on Mount Zion, but leave the pledge cards and the guilty consciences behind. No daily sacrifices are required; the one, perfect sacrifice has already been made. Down at Sinai, Abel's blood speaks a word of unfulfilled justice, but the only blood words spoken on Zion are these: 'This is my blood of the covenant, which is poured out for many for the forgiveness of sins" (12:24; see Matt, 26:28).

Zion Revisited (12:25–29)

Given the pictures of Sinai and Zion that the Preacher painted in the congregation's imagination, the travel decision is made. They are ready to order the tickets. Who would dare venture down the road to Sinai, a place of fire and noise, dire warnings and the shaking of the earth, when the other road leads to Zion, a place where there is singing in the streets and innumerable angels decked out like they are going to a fiesta?

But not so fast. The Preacher has a surprise left in his travelogue. He takes us back to Zion for a second look, and guess what? Mount Zion is also a place of fire and noise, stern warnings and the earth shaking. What is the Preacher saying? Is Mount Zion just Sinai with a little gingerbread—same old judgment, same old fear?

No, Zion and Sinai are an eternity apart; one is the mountain of the new covenant and other the old. It is true that, like Sinai, Zion has fire and shaking, but under the new covenant these experiences are transformed. Under the old order, fires and earthquakes are destroyers, burning up everything in their paths and shaking down all once-stable structures. Under the new covenant, though, God shakes heaven and earth like an antique collector shakes the dust off an old marble

139

statue: to get rid of everything that hides and defaces the beauty that was intended by the sculptor. In Zion, God shakes not to destroy but to preserve, "so that what cannot be shaken may remain" (12:27). In Zion, God is a consuming fire: not a wildfire burning out of control, but a refiner's fire, purifying and preserving the righteous (see Mal. 3:2–4), the fire that at the end of the age burns up "all causes of sin and evildoers" (see Matt. 13:40–43).

One important theological insight from this is that, for the Preacher, we do not have two Gods, one shrouded in smoke on Sinai, the other running around Zion like a dotty old man, twisting his watch fob and merrily handing out candy to children. The God of Sinai and the God of Zion are one and the same, holy and awe-full, a purifying fire of perfect judgment.

Is this good news, or bad? It depends upon whether we are gold or dross, the dust to be shaken off or the precious object that cannot be shaken. And if that depends upon us, then we are to be pitied. But the good news is that we do not go up on the mountain alone. Our older brother, the "firstborn" (1:5), goes with us, and he is the great high priest and "he is able for all time to save those who approach God through him" (7:25). He takes our dross and makes it gold; he takes us who are dust and makes us royal and holy, precious in the sight of God.

And that leads to a second theological insight: not only is there but one God; astonishingly, there is actually only one mountain. Sinai and Zion are the same place: the dwelling of the holy God. There *are* two paths, two ways to travel, but they both meet at the top of the same mountain. What makes the difference is not the destination, but the path; Mount Sinai is transformed into Mount Zion—if we go there with Jesus. Jesus lives on Mount Zion, and he is the royal Son. He spent "a little while" in the valley, " a little while . . . lower than the angels," and he suffered in every way as we. He did this not to help angels, but to show mercy to the descendants of Abraham (2:16), all of us who are wandering like "strangers and foreigners on the earth" (11:13), looking in vain for that city "whose architect and builder is God" (11:10). When his time had come, he cut a new path back up the hill, and he took us with him. He walked into the old sanctuary, now called "Zion," pulled back the curtain so all of us can come confidently in, and said to the God of the Ages, "I'm home, and I have brought the children with me" (2:10).

So the real question is not, "Where do you want to go today?" The real question is, "With whom will you travel?" On the path marked "Sinai," you travel on your own, and if you go to the mountain by yourself, on your own strength, you will not escape the judgment (12:25). But if we heed the voice speaking to us (12:25), the voice that "in these last days . . . has spoken to us by a Son" (1:1), then we will follow Christ into the heavenly tabernacle and "offer to God an acceptable worship with reverence and awe" (12:28).

This chapter ends with a powerful phrase: "Indeed our God is a consuming fire!" This statement is ambiguous. Should we sing the doxology or hide under the pew? The Preacher wants to leave the image undefined, since God's fire both refines and devours, purifies and incinerates. God's word is a two-edged sword (4:12), both severing and saving, and it all depends on whether or not we enter the sanctuary "by the new and living way that Jesus opened for us." The congregation must decide—as all must decide—whether to "shrink back" or to "have faith" (10:39), whether to drop fearfully and wearily away from the smoke and noise of the holy mountain or to "hold fast to our confession" (4:14) and "approach the throne of grace with boldness, so that we may receive mercy and find grace to help in time of need" (4:16).

So the words ring out and echo in the sanctuary: "Our God is a consuming fire." Apart from strengthening mercy, we are stubble and these are terrible words. But we are not apart from mercy, and these are, therefore, words of hope and a promise of holy and saving purification. The Preacher folds up his sermon notes now; there is more to come, but what follows are announcements and the benediction. But if the congregation were to sing a hymn here, it might be:

> Far off I see the goal—
> O Savior, guide me;
>
> I feel my strength is small—
> Be Thou beside me;
>
> With vision ever clear,
> With love that conquers fear,
>
> And grace to persevere,
> O Lord, provide me.
> (Robert R. Roberts)

Announcements and the Benediction

HEBREWS 13:1–21

Commentators have always noted the change in style that comes with chapter 13, some even wondering if the same person wrote this who composed the rest of Hebrews. There is, however, too much similarity—linguistically, thematically, theologically—to doubt a unified authorship (Attridge, *Hebrews*, p. 384).

What makes sense of the stylistic shift, though, is to recognize that the formal part of the Preacher's sermon is over. It concluded in the last chapter with the dramatic visit to Mount Zion and the stirring declaration that "Our God is a consuming fire" (12:18–29). The Preacher now turns to the more routine aspects of congregational life, to the ministry of hospitality, the prison visitation program, the stewardship emphasis, and the like. In short, the sermon is being followed by the announcements and the "joys and concerns." As is the case with all good preachers, however, the sermon actually continues. The preaching does not stop when the sermon notes are folded up, and the christological task does not end when the "minute for mission" begins.

The Announcements (13:1–19)

1. *Hospitality* (13:1–2). The first "announcement" has to do with simple hospitality. It is somehow comforting to know that the book in the New Testament with arguably the most elaborate christological doctrine brings it immediately home to the dinner table. It is almost as if the Preacher had said, "Because Jesus Christ, the firstborn of all time, the heir of all things is the great high priest who offered the perfect and lasting sacrifice and now sits in majesty at the right hand of God, therefore polish the silver and set the table for company."

Whenever the church shares a meal together—or any other aspect of its life—it is to continue to show "mutual love," that is, love for the other members of the congregation, one's fellow Christians, the "brothers and the sisters" (2:11). But this love should not be so ingrown that the church does not make a place at the table for the stranger, "for by doing that some have entertained angels without knowing it."

This allusion to entertaining angels unaware hearkens back to several Old Testament stories, especially the story of Abraham, Sarah, and the three strangers at Mamre (Gen. 18:1–15), but it also connects to Mount Zion. We are no longer merely having family night suppers at Shiloh Methodist, First Congregational, or Sacred Heart Cathedral; we are gathered for worship in the heavenly city where there are "innumerable angels" ready for the feast (12:22). They may look homeless and hungry when the church invites them into the warmth, but for those who have "the conviction of things not seen" (11:1), they bring the presence of God with them.

The third-century church order *Didascalia* gives instructions to bishops about the kind of ready hospitality they should show if a stranger should unexpectedly arrive at the assembly:

> If a destitute man or woman, either a local person or a traveler, arrives unexpectedly, especially one of older years, and there is no place, you, bishop, make such a place with all your heart, even if you yourself should sit on the ground, that you may not show favoritism among human beings, but that your ministry may be pleasing before God.

2. *Ministry with the Wounded* (12:3–4). The second "announcement" has to do with the prison ministry and the care of victims of torture and abuse. The church is not to engage in condescending charity but to provide a ministry of empathy, "as though you yourselves were in prison with them . . . as though you yourselves were being tortured." We do not do this because we are naturally compassionate, but as an imitation of Jesus, who entered so fully into the human situation that he is able "to sympathize with our weaknesses" (4:15) and, therefore, to supply the grace really to "help in time of need" (4:16).

3. *Sex and Money* (13:3–4). The Preacher, in this third group of announcements, goes from preaching to meddling. What he says about these two touchy topics is fairly conventional, namely that the community can be destroyed by love as much as by hate—loving the wrong person (fornication and adultery) and loving the wrong things (money).

What is not conventional is the christological grounding of these ethical values. The idea of the marriage bed being "defiled" is a purification concept, and thus it connects to the earlier discussion about Jesus, the great high priest, purifying our hearts and bodies (10:22). In short, fornication and adultery are not merely attacks on marriage and morality; they are denials of the sanctifying work of Christ.

As for money, the Preacher cites two Old Testament references—

143

"I will never leave you or forsake you" (probably a loose paraphrase of Deut. 31:6), and "The Lord is my helper; I will not be afraid . . ." (Ps. 118:6)—to support his directive to be content with what we have and not be acquisitive. What is inventive about this is, first, the suggestion that the love of money is not so much the product of greed as it is the fear of abandonment, and two, the intriguing theological claim that when Jesus Christ grasps our one hand in love it frees us to open up the clenched other one and let the money go.

4. *Worship and Service* (12:7–17). This very difficult section is marked off at the beginning and the end with a word about following their leaders. We cannot tell exactly what was happening in the Preacher's congregation, but at least some members of the church were getting off the track and needed the corrective guidance of "the leaders." This prompts the preacher to put down the announcement insert and to re-preach part of his sermon.

We can see two main features of the problem.

a. First, some in the congregation were confusing grace with regulations, in their case evidently some sort of rules regarding food (12:9). The Preacher reminds them that people eat food, not etiquette, and in the Christian community people are nourished by grace, not by regulations (13:9).

Indeed, the whole attempt to turn Christianity into a rule-based ritualistic religion is, in the Preacher's view, a failure of nerve, a shrinking back (10:29) from the bold approach to the heavenly sanctuary made possible in Christ. It is, in effect, to return to that old tent where the old priest gave old sacrifices that were of no benefit to those who observed them (13:9; see 9:6–10, esp. 9:9).

The remedy for that, of course, is to go to the new place of sacrifice—to leave the old tent with its ineffective sacrifices and to go where the everlasting and truly cleansing sacrifice is made. And that is exactly where the Preacher takes us: "We have an altar . . ." he begins, emphasizing the "we" and pointing his finger toward the cross, an altar to which those who operate by the old covenant, the old law, the religion of rules and perpetual sacrifices, have no access, "no right to eat" (13:10; some see here a reference to the Eucharist, but that is not clear and certainly not necessary to the argument). If you want to get there, though, if you want to go to the place where the true sacrifice was offered once for all, the path will take you "outside the camp." The use of that phrase allows us to see the second part of the problem:

b. The congregation has a problem with the public side, the "outside the camp" dimension, of the Christian faith. Some are not even coming to worship (10:25), but even those who do are reluctant to show their Christian faces out in the world. One can hardly blame them; when they stick their heads outside of the sanctuary door they are liable to be "publicly exposed to abuse and persecution" (see comments on 10:32–39). Small wonder then that they would like to redefine the Christian faith as a list of food rules rather than as a comprehensive way of life.

"But," says the Preacher, "we have this altar," and the only way to get there is to leave the safe confines of the camp and go outside the city wall. Here the Preacher blends two traditions. One, from Leviticus 16:27, describes how the sacrificial animals whose blood was used in the old sanctuary were burned outside the camp, and the other, from the early church's tradition, indicates that Jesus was crucified outside of the city walls (see John 19:17–20). The point, however, is not so much the complicated analogy between the two traditions but the missional mandate. If Jesus went outside and suffered public abuse in order to make *his* sacrifice, then his brothers and sisters should be willing to follow him to make ours.

This whole section began by urging the congregation to "remember your leaders who spoke the word of God to you," and Jesus, after all, is the first and quintessential leader who spoke the word to us. We are supposed to "consider the outcome of their way of life and imitate their faith." This means, in Jesus' case—since he is the same yesterday and today and forever (13:8)—going right outside the camp, facing the same abuse he faced, and making our sacrifice (13:13).

We do not make, of course, the same sacrifice that Jesus offered; his was "once for all" (10:10). Our sacrifices are praising God, confessing God's name in public, doing works of mercy, and sharing what we have with others (13:15–16)—in other words, right out there in public view we are to worship, evangelize, empathetically serve the needy, and exercise generosity to others. Such "sacrifices are pleasing to God" (13:16), which is one of the marks of faith (11:6).

For any in the congregation who protest that they are quite content "inside the walls," thank you, the Preacher reminds them that they are setting up residence in the wrong city. "For here we have no lasting city, but we are looking for the city that is to come" (13:14, see 11:10). This may sound scary, but it is actually freeing and reassuring. We go to a homeland that cannot be shaken, to receive an inheritance that cannot be stolen. This means that the faithful can go outside the camp boldly, courageously, and with all good cheer, not engaging in destructive murmurs and fearful sighs (13:17). What the Preacher said about money applies to the whole of the Christian life and mission: "I will not be afraid. What can anyone do to me?" (13:6) Now there's a "minute for mission"!

5. *Prayer Request* (13:18–19). The service is nearly over now. People are pulling on their coats, and as a parting word in worship the Preacher asks for prayer for himself. "I've done the best I can, and I have a clear conscience" (13:18). The Preacher particularly asks for traveling prayers, since he hopes to be "restored" to them "very soon" (13:19). This is a clue that the Preacher is not an outsider, but a member of the community temporarily separated from them. Perhaps he is one of the itinerant preachers who traveled from place to place in the early church. We do not know for sure, but he again picks up the idea of visiting them in 13:23.

The Benediction (13:20–21)

Now the Preacher figuratively raises his hands over the flock to give the blessing to those who have listened to his sermon. This benediction is no afterthought but reflects some of the key theological emphases of the sermon. Indeed, each phrase is loaded with meaning drawn from the overall sermon:

The God of peace (13:20). God is the God of peace in ways small and large. God is the author of the smaller forms of peace found when the community lets "mutual love continue," but this finally flows in and out of the larger peace established between God and humanity by the work of the great high priest (see 7:1—10:39).

Who brought back from the dead our Lord Jesus Christ (13:20). The Preacher uses an unusual Greek work in describing the resurrection. Instead of the typical "raised," the verb is a word meaning "led out" or "led up." So the Preacher's benediction actually speaks of the God "who led up Jesus from the dead." The phrase is significant since it recalls the repeated picture in Hebrews of the "parabola of salvation" (see comment on 1:5–14). Jesus travels from the heavenly realm downward through time and space into the place of suffering, and then is "led up" by God, holding fast to his brothers and sisters, and bringing them with him into the heavenly sanctuary.

The great shepherd of the sheep (13:20). The picture of God "leading up" Jesus from death flows into the accompanying image of Jesus leading his followers. The shepherd imagery, though not the Preacher's usual way of speaking, does convey the idea of the faithful being led to the safety and nourishment of green pastures.

By the blood of the eternal covenant (13:20). This phrase is short-

146

hand for the great high-priestly ministry of Jesus and the new covenant he established by his perfect sacrifice, themes which the Preacher developed at significant length in the sermon (see comments on 8:1—9:28).

Make you complete in everything good, so that you may do his will (13:21). This phrase again refers to the high-priestly ministry of Jesus, who by his perfect sacrifice on our behalf made us whole, complete, sanctified. We were created in the image of God, and it was Jesus who offered his own life, tested but sinless, and brought that intention to its full and fruitful end. "For by a single offering he has perfected for all time those who are sanctified" (10:14). Those who are joined to him by faith are empowered to "do his will" in offering praise to God and compassionate service to others (see 13:15–16).

Working among us that which is pleasing in his sight (13:21). Like many benedictions, this one has so many clauses that it is sometimes difficult to tell who is the subject of what verb. In this case it is *God* who "works among us that which is pleasing in his [that is, in God's] sight." This presents the intriguing picture of God at work in human life doing things to please himself. However awkward this may be grammatically, it is elegant theologically. Just as God in the beginning looked at the first human beings, as well as all else in creation, and called them "very good," now God in Jesus Christ makes of human beings a "new creation," and it, too, is "very good."

What is it that is "pleasing in God's sight"? Earlier the Preacher told us that "without faith it is impossible to please God" (11:6). Now it becomes clear that all those works of mercy, acts of courage, expressions of hope, and risks of love—things that proceed from faith—indeed faith itself—are gifts from God, signs that God is "at work" in us.

Through Jesus Christ, to whom be the glory forever and ever. Amen (13:21). This beautiful benediction ends where the sermon began, with Jesus in glory, seated "at the right hand of the Majesty on high" (1:3).

Final Notes

HEBREWS 13:22–25

Hebrews is a sermon, as we have observed all along. But it is a sermon that was preached *in absentia*, and when it was sent to the congregation, certain "epistle-like" additions were posted to the end. In the first of these "final notes," the Preacher requests that the congregation bear with his "exhortation" (a word sometimes to describe sermons), because it is, after all, "brief." In comparison to other New Testament letters, Hebrews is not all that brief (in fact, except for Romans and 1 Corinthians, Hebrews is the longest New Testament letter), but in the ancient world it was a polite convention among the educated to call the letters, regardless of their length, "brief." We have here, then, one more sign of the culture and sophistication of the Preacher.

The congregation knows "Timothy," who is probably the same one mentioned in connection to Paul (see, for example, Acts 16:1–3; 2 Cor. 1:1, 19), and they were probably aware of his circumstances. But we are not, and so it is not clear whether his being "set free" should be taken as a reference to prison (probably) or to other commitments (possibly). In any case, the Preacher hopes that Timothy will accompany him when he visits the congregation, and the naming of Timothy puts our Preacher at least on the outer edges of the Pauline circle.

The last note, in which greetings are exchanged, has always stimulated excited speculation about the geography of Hebrews, but its accurate meaning is frustratingly elusive. After sending greetings to the whole congregation ("Greet all your leaders and all the saints"), the Preacher says something about "those from Italy" also sending greetings. This means that some Italians have sent greetings to the congregation. But is this because the Preacher is *in* Italy and writing, "All the Christians around here in Italy send you greetings"? Or is it because he is in some unknown place and writing home *to* Italy, saying "All the homesick Italians here with me send greetings and wish they were there"? Or perhaps the Preacher is in some unknown spot writing to the congregation in an equally unknown locale and simply saying, "I am here with some Italians and they want me to say hello." Take your pick.

The geographical location of Hebrews may be obscure, but its

148

theological location is not. We do not know where the Preacher is on the globe, but we do know where he stands on the map of faith. The last line of Hebrews tells everything: "Grace be with all of you."

Of course, this is in some ways a standard farewell, but in other ways it sums up the message the Preacher has proclaimed to his congregation. Whether they are in Italy or Greece, Antioch or Alexandria, Chicago, or Bangkok, grace will find them—all of them—and dwell with them. That is the ultimate message of Hebrews, the ultimate message of the gospel. Because of the ministry of the great high priest, the great shepherd of the sheep, grace is with all of you . . . everywhere.

BIBLIOGRAPHY

For further study

Attridge, Harold W. *The Epistle to the Hebrews.* Philadelphia: Fortress Press, 1989.

Ellingworth, Paul. *The Epistle to the Hebrews.* London: Epworth Press, 1991.

Ellingworth, Paul and Eugene Nida. *A Translator's Handbook on the Letter to the Hebrews.* London: United Bible Societies, 1983.

Hay, David M. *Glory at the Right Hand: Psalm 110 in Early Christianity.* Nashville: Abingdon Press, 1973.

Hurst, L. D. *The Epistle to the Hebrews: Its Background of Thought.* Cambridge: Cambridge University Press, 1990.

Jewett, Robert. *Letter to Pilgrims: A Commentary on the Epistle to the Hebrews.* New York: Pilgrim Press, 1981.

Lane, William L. *Hebrews 1—8.* Dallas: Word Books, 1991.

Lane, William L. *Hebrews 9—13.* Dallas: Word Books, 1991.

Lindars, Barnabas. *The Theology of the Letter to the Hebrews.* New York: Cambridge University Press, 1991.

Wilson, R. McL. *Hebrews.* Grand Rapids: Wm. B. Eerdmans Publishing Co., 1987.

Literature cited

Allen, Woody. *Without Feathers.* New York: Random House, 1975.

Attridge, Harold W. *The Epistle to the Hebrews.* Philadelphia: Fortress Press, 1989.

Auden, W. H. *Collected Poems.* New York: Random House, 1976.

Bellow, Saul. *Mr. Sammler's Planet.* New York: Viking Press, 1970.

Berry, Wendell. *Collected Poems, 1957–82.* Berkeley, Calif.: North Point Press, 1985.

Bondi, Roberta C. *Memories of God: Theological Reflections on a Life.* Nashville: Abingdon Press, 1995.

Buechner, Frederick. *Wishful Thinking: A Theological ABC.* New York: Harper & Row, 1973.

Buttrick, David G. "Up against the Powers That Be." In *A Chorus of Witnesses: Model Sermons for Today's Preacher,* edited by Thomas G. Long and Cornelius Plantinga, Jr. Grand Rapids: Wm. B. Eerdmans Publishing Co., 1994, pp. 218–24.

Ellingworth, Paul. *The Epistle to the Hebrews.* London: Epworth Press, 1991.

Ellingworth, Paul, and Eugene Nida. *A Translator's Handbook on the Letter to the Hebrews.* London: United Bible Societies, 1983.

Garrow, David J. *Bearing the Cross: Martin Luther King, Jr. and the Southern Christian Leadership Conference.* New York: Viking Penguin, 1986.

Hall, Douglas John. *Professing the Faith: Christian Theology in a North American Context.* Minneapolis: Fortress Press, 1993.

Hay, David M. *Glory at the Right Hand: Psalm 110 in Early Christianity.* Nashville: Abingdon Press, 1973.

Hurst, L. D. *The Epistle to the Hebrews: Its Background of Thought.* Cambridge: Cambridge University Press, 1990.

Jewett, Robert. *Letter to Pilgrims: A Commentary on the Epistle to the Hebrews.* New York: Pilgrim Press, 1981.

Johnson, Luke T. *The Writings of the New Testament: An Interpretation.* Philadelphia: Fortress Press, 1986.

Keizer, Garret. *A Dresser of Sycamore Trees: The Finding of a Ministry.* New York: Viking Penguin, 1991.

Kozol, Jonathan. *Amazing Grace: The Lives of Children and the Conscience of a Nation.* New York: HarperCollins, 1996.

Küng, Hans. *On Being a Christian.* Garden City, N.Y.: Doubleday & Co., 1976.

Lane, William L. *Hebrews 1—8.* Dallas: Word Books, 1991.

Lane, William L. *Hebrews 9—13.* Dallas: Word Books, 1991.

Lewis, C. S. *The Screwtape Letters.* New York: Macmillan Co., 1962.

Lindars, Barnabas. *The Theology of the Letter to the Hebrews.* New York: Cambridge University Press, 1991.

Lindsay, Vachel. "General William Booth Enters into Heaven." In *Masterpieces of Religious Verse,* ed. James Dalton Morrison. New York: Harper & Brothers, 1948.

Michener, James A. *Iberia: Spanish Travels and Reflections.* New York: Random House, 1968.

Migliore, Daniel. *Faith Seeking Understanding: An Introduction to Christian Theology.* Grand Rapids: Wm. B. Eerdmans Publishing Co., 1991.

Morse, Christopher. *Not Every Spirit: A Dogmatics of Christian Unbelief.* Valley Forge, Pa.: Trinity Press, 1994.

Ong, Walter J. *Orality and Literacy: The Technologizing of the Word.* London: Methuen, 1982.

Placher, William C. "The Acts of God: What Do We Mean by Revelation?" *Christian Century,* March 20–27, 1996, pp. 337–42.

Simon, Ernst. "Martin Buber: His Way Between Thought and Deed." *Jewish Frontier* 15 (1948).

Stoppard, Tom. *The Real Thing*. Boston: Faber & Faber, 1984.

Sweet, Leonard I. *Strong in the Broken Places: A Theological Reverie on the Ministry of George Everett Ross*. Akron, Ohio: University of Akron Press, 1995.

Taylor, Barbara Brown. *The Preaching Life*. Cambridge, Mass.: Cowley Publications, 1993.

Wilson, R. McL. *Hebrews*. Grand Rapids: Wm. B. Eerdmans Publishing Co., 1987.

CPSIA information can be obtained
at www.ICGtesting.com
Printed in the USA
LVHW031347150421
684544LV00012B/80